COMMON CORE

MATH

Activities that Captivate, Motivate, and Reinforce

Grade 8

by Marjorie Frank

IncentivePublications

BY WORLD BOOK

a Scott Fetzer company

Illustrated by Kathleen Bullock
Cover by Penny Laporte

Print Edition ISBN 978-1-62950-239-7
E-book Edition ISBN 978-1-62950-240-3 (PDF)

World Book, Inc.
233 North Michigan Avenue
Suite 2000
Chicago, Illinois 60601 U.S.A.

For information about World Book and Incentive Publications products, call **1-800-967-5325,** or visit our websites at **www.worldbook.com** and **www.incentivepublications.com.**

Printed in the United States of America by Sheridan Books, Inc.
Chelsea, Michigan
1st Printing August 2014

CONTENTS

Introduction

Grade 8 Common Core State Standards for Mathematics

The Number System

Expressions and Equations

Functions

Geometry

Statistics and Probability

Assessment and Answer Keys

Great Support for Common Core State Standards!

Invite your students to join in on curious and quirky adventures with all kinds of sports—including some as unusual as flying out of a cannon or fire walking! They will delight in the high-appeal topics and the many inventive math uses. They can

. . . marvel at the statistics in the life of a human cannonball;

. . . drop in on some candlestick-jumping competitions;

. . . discover the math connection between caffeine and falling asleep in class;

. . . cheer on racing worms, lizards, turtles, and cockroaches;

. . . use the Pythagorean Theorem to avoid a dangerous underwater confrontation;

. . . figure out how functions can help a Wild West cowboy get out of town fast;

. . . put geometry to use in the ice cream shop, pizza parlor, and locker room;

. . . measure distances that people throw such things as running chainsaws, cell phones, DVDs, Christmas trees, or rubber chickens;

. . . clean up homework that got messed up in a paintball fight;

. . . solve a brain-busting equation in time to help a skateboarder survive Bonebreaker Boulevard;

. . . and tackle many other delightful tasks.

And while they engage in these adventures, they will be moving toward competence in critical math skills that they need for success in the real world.

How to Use This Book

- The pages are tools to support your teaching of the concepts, processes, and skills outlined in the Common Core State Standards. This is not a curriculum; it is a collection of engaging experiences for you to use as you do math with your students or children.

- Use any given page to introduce, explain, teach, practice, extend, assess, provide independent work, start a discussion about, or get students collaborating on a skill or concept.

- Use any page in a large-group or small-group setting to deepen understandings and expand knowledge and skills.

- Pages are not intended for use solely as independent work. Do the activities together or review and discuss the work together.

- Each activity is focused on a particular standard, but most make use of or can be expanded to strengthen other standards as well.

- The book is organized according to the Common Core math domains. Use the tables on pages 9 to 16, the page labels, and notations on the Contents pages to identify the standards supported by each page.

- For further mastery of Common Core State Standards, use the suggestions on page 8.

About Common Core State Standards for Mathematics

The Common Core State Standards for Mathematics at the middle-grades level aim to expand conceptual understanding of the key ideas of math while they strengthen foundational skills, operations, and principles. They identify what students should know, understand, and be able to do—with an emphasis on explaining principles and applying them to a wide range of situations. To best help students achieve these robust standards for math . . .

1. Know the standards well. Keep them in front of you. Understand for yourself the big picture of what the standards seek to do. (See www.corestandards.org.)

2. Work to apply, expand, and deepen student skills. With activities in this book (or any learning activities), plan to include
   . . . interaction with peers in pairs, small groups, and large groups
   . . . plenty of discussion, integration, and hands-on work with math concepts
   . . . questioning, analyzing, modeling math situations, explaining what you are doing and thinking, using tools effectively, and applying to real-world problems
   . . . lots of observation, meaningful feedback, follow-up, and reflection.

3. Ask questions that advance reasoning, application, and real-life connection:
   - *What, exactly, IS the problem?*
   - *How could you solve this another way?*
   - *Does this make sense? (Why or why not?)*
   - *How could you state the problem in a different way?*
   - *What information is needed to solve this problem?*
   - *What information in the problem is not needed?*
   - *What operations do you need to use?*
   - *If we change ____, what will happen to ____?*
   - *What tools do you need to solve this?*
   - *How could you illustrate your problem-solving process?*
   - *What did you learn from solving this problem?*
   - *When could you use this? Where could you use this?*
   - *How did you arrive at your answer?*
   - *How can you show that your answer is right?*
   - *Where else have you seen a problem like this?*
   - *What does this ask you to do?*
   - *What led you to this conclusion?*
   - *How could we figure this out?*
   - *What was the first step you took?*
   - *How could you make a model of this?*
   - *How could you demonstrate your solution?*
   - *If ____ changed, how would the solution change?*
   - *What patterns do you notice?*
   - *Where have you seen this in real life?*
   - *What does this remind you of?*
   - *What could be another answer?*
   - *How could you show this a different way?*
   - *If this is true, then what else might be true?*
   - *How can you explain your answer?*
   - *How could you ask that question differently?*
   - *What will you do next?*

Standards for Mathematical Practice, Grades K-12

Math Practice Standard	Standard	Pages that Support
MP1	Make sense of problems and persevere in solving them.	18-26, 28-58, 60-74, 76-110, 112-126
MP2	Reason abstractly and quantitatively.	18-26, 28-58, 60-74, 76-110, 112-126
MP3	Construct viable arguments and critique the reasoning of others.	19, 20-21, 24-25, 26, 28, 29, 31, 32, 35, 39, 42, 47, 49, 51, 53, 60-74, 78-110, 112-126
MP4	Model with mathematics.	22, 24-25, 26, 29, 40-41, 42, 43-45, 51, 54-55, 60-74, 76-110, 112-126
MP5	Use appropriate tools strategically.	18-26, 28-58, 60-74, 76-110, 112-126
MP6	Attend to precision.	18-26, 28-58, 60-74, 76-110, 112-126
MP7	Look for and make use of structure.	18-26, 28-58, 60-74, 76-110, 112-126
MP8	Look for and express regularity in repeated reasoning.	20-21, 22, 24-25, 26, 28-58, 60-74, 76-110, 112-126

Grade 8 Common Core State Standards for Mathematical Content

8.NS.A The Number System

Math Content Standard	Standard	Pages that Support
Know that there are numbers that are not rational, and approximate them by rational numbers.		
8.NS.A.1	Know that numbers that are not rational are called irrational. Understand informally that every number has a decimal expansion; for rational numbers show that the decimal expansion repeats eventually, and convert a decimal expansion which repeats eventually into a rational number.	18, 19, 20-21, 22, 23, 24-25, 26
8.NS.A.2	Use rational approximations of irrational numbers to compare the size of irrational numbers, locate them approximately on a number line diagram, and estimate the value of expressions (e.g., π^2). *For example, by truncating the decimal expansion of $\sqrt{2}$, show that $\sqrt{2}$ is between 1 and 2, then between 1.4 and 1.5, and explain how to continue on to get better approximations.*	23, 24-25, 26

Grade 8 Common Core State Standards for Mathematical Content

8.EE   Expressions and Equations

Math Content Standard	Standard	Pages that Support
8.EE.A	**Expressions and equations work with radicals and integer exponents.**	
8.EE.A.1	Know and apply the properties of integer exponents to generate equivalent numerical expressions. For example, $3^2 \times 3^{-5} = 3^{-3} = (\frac{1}{3})^3 = \frac{1}{27}$.	28, 29, 30, 31, 32, 33, 34, 35, 36, 37, 38, 39
8.EE.A.2	Use square root and cube root symbols to represent solutions to equations of the form $x^2 = p$ and $x^3 = p$, where p is a positive rational number. Evaluate square roots of small perfect squares and cube roots of small perfect cubes. Know that $\sqrt{2}$ is irrational.	33, 34, 35
8.EE.A.3	Use numbers expressed in the form of a single digit times an integer power of 10 to estimate very large or very small quantities, and to express how many times as much one is than the other. *For example, estimate the population of the United States as 3 times 108 and the population of the world as 7 times 109, and determine that the world population is more than 20 times larger.*	36, 37, 38, 39
8.EE.A.4	Perform operations with numbers expressed in scientific notation, including problems where both decimal and scientific notation are used. Use scientific notation and choose units of appropriate size for measurements of very large or very small quantities (e.g., use millimeters per year for seafloor spreading). Interpret scientific notation that has been generated by technology.	36, 37, 38, 39
8.EE.B	**Understand the connections between proportional relationships, lines, and linear equations.**	
8.EE.B.5	Graph proportional relationships, interpreting the unit rate as the slope of the graph. Compare two different proportional relationships represented in different ways. *For example, compare a distance-time graph to a distance-time equation to determine which of two moving objects has greater speed.*	40-41, 42, 43-45
8.EE.B.6	Use similar triangles to explain why the slope m is the same between any two distinct points on a nonvertical line in the coordinate plane; derive the equation $y = mx$ for a line through the origin and the equation $y = mx + b$ for a line intercepting the vertical axis at b.	43-45

Grade 8 Expressions and Equations Standards continue on next page.

Common Core Reinforcement Activities — 8th Grade Math

Grade 8 Common Core State Standards for Mathematical Content

8.EE   Expressions and Equations, continued

Math Content Standard	Standard	Pages that Support
8.EE.C	**Analyze and solve linear equations and pairs of simultaneous linear equations.**	
8.EE.C.7	Solve linear equations in one variable.	46-52
8.EE.C.7a	Give examples of linear equations in one variable with one solution, infinitely many solutions, or no solutions. Show which of these possibilities is the case by successively transforming the given equation into simpler forms, until an equivalent equation of the form $x = a$, $a = a$, or $a = b$ results (where a and b are different numbers).	46-47, 48, 49, 50, 51, 52
8.EE.C.7b	Solve linear equations with rational number coefficients, including equations whose solutions require expanding expressions using the distributive property and collecting like terms.	46-47, 48, 49, 50, 51, 52
8.EE.C.8	Analyze and solve pairs of simultaneous linear equations.	53-58
8.EE.C.8a	Understand that solutions to a system of two linear equations in two variables correspond to points of intersection of their graphs, because points of intersection satisfy both equations simultaneously.	53, 54-55, 56, 57, 58
8.EE.C.8b	Solve systems of two linear equations in two variables algebraically, and estimate solutions by graphing the equations. Solve simple cases by inspection. *For example, $3x + 2y = 5$ and $3x + 2y = 6$ have no solution because $3x + 2y$ cannot simultaneously be 5 and 6.*	53, 54-55, 58
8.EE.C.8c	Solve real-world and mathematical problems leading to two linear equations in two variables. *For example, given coordinates for two pairs of points, determine whether the line through the first pair of points intersects the line through the second pair.*	54-55, 56, 57, 58

Grade 8 Common Core State Standards for Mathematical Content

8.F   Functions

Math Content Standard	Standard	Pages that Support
8.EE.C	**Use properties of operations to generate equivalent expressions.**	
8.F.A.1	Understand that a function is a rule that assigns to each input exactly one output. The graph of a function is the set of ordered pairs consisting of an input and the corresponding output.	60-61, 62-63, 64, 65-67, 68, 70, 71, 72, 73, 74
8.F.A.2	Compare properties of two functions each represented in a different way (algebraically, graphically, numerically in tables, or by verbal descriptions). For example, given a linear function represented by a table of values and a linear function represented by an algebraic expression, determine which function has the greater rate of change.	60-61, 62-63, 64, 65-67
8.F.A.3	Interpret the equation $y = mx + b$ as defining a linear function whose graph is a straight line; give examples of functions that are not linear. *For example, the function $A = s^2$ giving the area of a square as a function of its side length is not linear because its graph contains the points (1,1), (2,4), and (3,9), which are not on a straight line.*	68, 69, 70, 71, 72, 73
8.F.B	**Use functions to model relationships between quantities.**	
8.F.B.4	Construct a function to model a linear relationship between two quantities. Determine the rate of change and initial value of the function from a description of a relationship or from two (x, y) values, including reading these from a table or from a graph. Interpret the rate of change and initial value of a linear function in terms of the situation it models and in terms of its graph or a table of values.	69, 70, 71, 72, 73
8.F.B.5	Describe qualitatively the functional relationship between two quantities by analyzing a graph (e.g., where the function is increasing or decreasing, linear or nonlinear). Sketch a graph that exhibits the qualitative features of a function that has been described verbally.	74

Grade 8 Common Core State Standards for Mathematical Content

8.G   Geometry

Math Content Standard	Standard	Pages that Support
8.G.A	**Understand congruence and similarity using physical models, transparencies, or geometry software.**	
8.G.A.1	Verify experimentally the properties of rotations, reflections, and translations.	76-85
8.G.A.1a	Lines are taken to lines, and line segments to line segments of the same length.	76-77, 78-79, 80, 81, 84-85
8.G.A.1b	Angles are taken to angles of the same measure.	76-77, 81, 82-83
8.G.A.1c	Parallel lines are taken to parallel lines.	76-77, 84-85
8.G.A.2	Understand that a two-dimensional figure is congruent to another if the second can be obtained from the first by a sequence of rotations, reflections, and translations; given two congruent figures, describe a sequence that exhibits the congruence between them.	76-77, 86-87, 88-89
8.G.A.3	Describe the effect of dilations, translations, rotations, and reflections on two-dimensional figures using coordinates.	76-77, 90-91
8.G.A.4	Understand that a two-dimensional figure is similar to another if the second can be obtained from the first by a sequence of rotations, reflections, translations, and dilations; given two similar two-dimensional figures, describe a sequence that exhibits the similarity between them.	76-77, 92-93
8.G.A.5	Use informal arguments to establish facts about the angle sum and exterior angle of triangles, about the angles created when parallel lines are cut by a transversal, and the angle-angle criterion for similarity of triangles. *For example, arrange three copies of the same triangle so that the sum of the three angles appears to form a line, and give an argument in terms of transversals why this is so.*	76-77, 94, 95

Grade 8 Geometry Standards continue on next page.

Grade 8 Common Core State Standards for Mathematical Content

8.G   Geometry, continued

Math Content Standard	Standard	Pages that Support
8.G.B	**Understand and apply the Pythagorean Theorem.**	
8.G.B.6	Explain a proof of the Pythagorean Theorem and its converse.	98, 99
8.G.B.7	Apply the Pythagorean Theorem to determine unknown side lengths in right triangles in real-world and mathematical problems in two and three dimensions.	100, 101, 102-103, 104-105
8.G.B.8	Apply the Pythagorean Theorem to find the distance between two points in a coordinate system.	104-105
8.G.C	**Solve real-world and mathematical problems involving volume of cylinders, cones, and spheres.**	
8.G.C.9	Know the formulas for the volumes of cones, cylinders, and spheres and use them to solve real-world and mathematical problems.	106-107, 108-109, 110

Grade 8 Common Core State Standards for Mathematical Content

8.SP   Statistics and Probability

Math Content Standard	Standard	Pages that Support
8.SP.A	**Investigate patterns of association in bivariate data.**	
8.SP.A.1	Construct and interpret scatter plots for bivariate measurement data to investigate patterns of association between two quantities. Describe patterns such as clustering, outliers, positive or negative association, linear association, and nonlinear association.	112, 113, 114-115, 116-117, 118, 119, 120, 121, 122
8.SP.A.2	Know that straight lines are widely used to model relationships between two quantitative variables. For scatter plots that suggest a linear association, informally fit a straight line, and informally assess the model fit by judging the closeness of the data points to the line.	116-117, 118, 119, 120, 121, 122
8.SP.A.3	Use the equation of a linear model to solve problems in the context of bivariate measurement data, interpreting the slope and intercept. *For example, in a linear model for a biology experiment, interpret a slope of 1.5 cm/hr as meaning that an additional hour of sunlight each day is associated with an additional 1.5 cm in mature plant height.*	118, 119, 120, 121, 122
8.SP.A.4	Understand that patterns of association can also be seen in bivariate categorical data by displaying frequencies and relative frequencies in a two-way table. Construct and interpret a two-way table summarizing data on two categorical variables collected from the same subjects. Use relative frequencies calculated for rows or columns to describe possible association between the two variables. *For example, collect data from students in your class on whether or not they have a curfew on school nights and whether or not they have assigned chores at home. Is there evidence that those who have a curfew also tend to have chores?*	123, 124, 125, 126

16

RATIOS
AND
PROPORTIONAL
RELATIONSHIPS

Grade 8

$$\int_{-\infty}^{\infty} e^{-x^2} dx = \sqrt{\pi}$$

WATCH THOSE FLAGS!

Marilee is a mathematical slalom skier. On this course, she must pass through gates with irrational numbers. This means that if there is not an irrational number on the flag to each side of her as she passes through a row of flags, she will be disqualified.

Draw a path down the mountain from START to FINISH for Marilee.

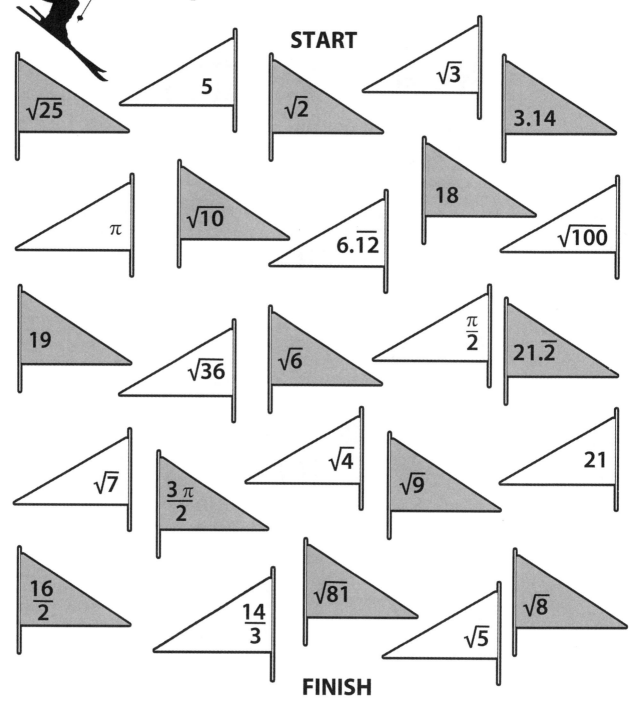

THE SPORT OF NUMBERS

$$\int_{-\infty}^{\infty} e^{-x^2}\,dx = \sqrt{\pi}$$

Not all sports involve body action. Many people enjoy mind sports, including sports that involve playing with numbers. 13-year old Priyanshi Somani, of India, has competed in international mind sports since she was 10 years old. In 2012, she set a record for the fastest calculation of six-digit square roots. One could say she's a whiz with rational and irrational numbers!

Show some of your brilliance with irrational and rational numbers by identifying each statement as true (T) or false (F).

_____ 1. The expression $\sqrt{(x + 2)^4}$ could represent a rational number or an irrational number.

_____ 2. The sum of two rational numbers is a rational number.

_____ 3. Every rational number is an integer.

_____ 4. All integers are rational numbers.

_____ 5. The decimal expansion of an irrational number never repeats or terminates.

_____ 6. $\frac{1}{\sqrt{2}}$ is an irrational number.

_____ 7. $\sqrt{2} - \sqrt{2}$ is an irrational number.

_____ 8. $\sqrt{(13)^4}$ is an irrational number.

_____ 9. Any fraction with a radical in the denominator is irrational.

_____ 10. The cube root of 64 is a rational number.

_____ 11. 137^5 is an irrational number.

_____ 12. π multiplied by a rational number will yield an irrational number.

_____ 13. All repeating decimals are irrational numbers.

_____ 14. $\frac{\pi}{\pi}$ is an irrational number.

Name

JERSEY MIX-UP

Two teams with unusual names (the Rationals and the Irrationals) face each other in the league playoffs. But both teams are having jersey trouble! Several jerseys ended up in the wrong locker room. Of course, the Rationals should have jerseys with rational numbers and the Irrationals should have jerseys with irrational numbers. You'll need to straighten out this mess.

Examine the jerseys now in the possession of each team. Use red to shade the jerseys that belong to the Rationals. Use blue to shade the jerseys that belong to the Irrationals. Circle the jerseys that are on the wrong page (the jerseys that belong to the Irrationals).

The Rationals

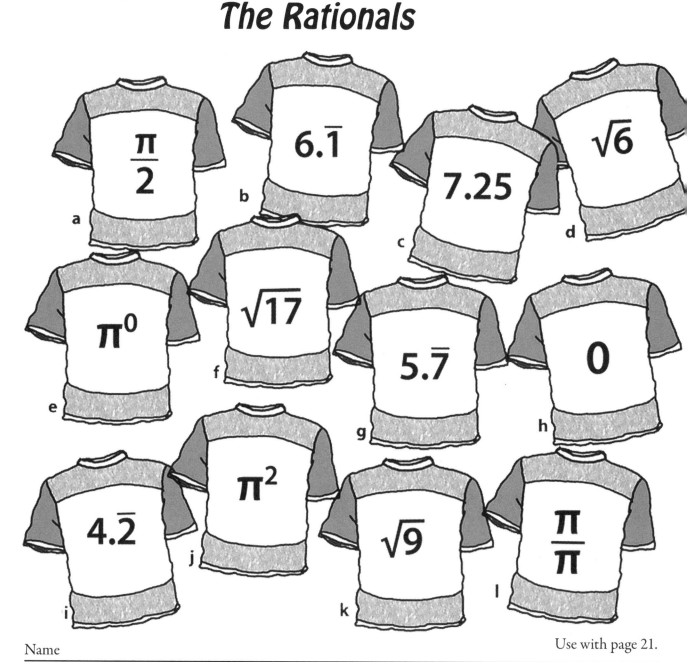

Examine the jerseys now in the possession of each team. (See page 20.) Use blue to shade the jerseys that belong to the Irrationals. Use red to shade the jerseys that belong to the Rationals. Circle the jerseys that are on the wrong page (the jerseys that belong to the Rationals).

The Irrationals

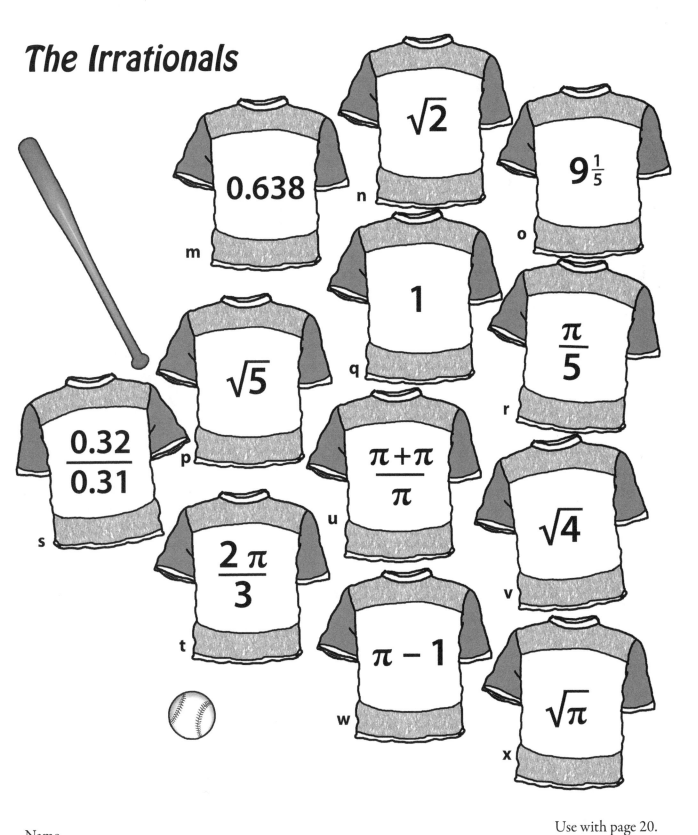

m. 0.638

n. $\sqrt{2}$

o. $9\frac{1}{5}$

q. 1

r. $\dfrac{\pi}{5}$

p. $\sqrt{5}$

s. $\dfrac{0.32}{0.31}$

u. $\dfrac{\pi+\pi}{\pi}$

v. $\sqrt{4}$

t. $\dfrac{2\pi}{3}$

w. $\pi-1$

x. $\sqrt{\pi}$

Name

Use with page 20.

EXTREME EATING

One unusual sport may seem tasty to some or distasteful to others. It's the sport of competitive eating. The International Federation of Competitive Eating keeps records of speed-eating feats. Competitors join together in speed-eating contests of all kinds—racing to eat such things as ice cream, crawfish, deep-fried asparagus, hard-boiled eggs, and dozens of other foods. (Don't try these contests at home!)

For problems 1-3, answer the questions about rational numbers.

1

Which of the following is not a way to write the rational number $\frac{9}{4}$?

a. $2 + \frac{1}{4}$

b. $\sqrt{\frac{81}{16}}$

c. $\frac{9\pi}{4\pi}$

d. $(1.5)^2$

e. 2.25

f. $\frac{9\pi}{4}$

2

Which of the following is not a way to write the rational number $\frac{7}{5}$?

a. 1.4

b. 0.714285

c. $\sqrt{\frac{49}{25}}$

d. $\frac{14\pi}{10\pi}$

e. $\sqrt{1.96}$

f. $1 + \frac{2}{5}$

3. What is wrong with this definition? A real number (r) is rational if and only if there exist integers **a** and **b** such that $r = \frac{a}{b}$

For problems 4-10, each of the repeating decimals can be written as a ratio of two integers. Draw a line to the food with the matching ratio.

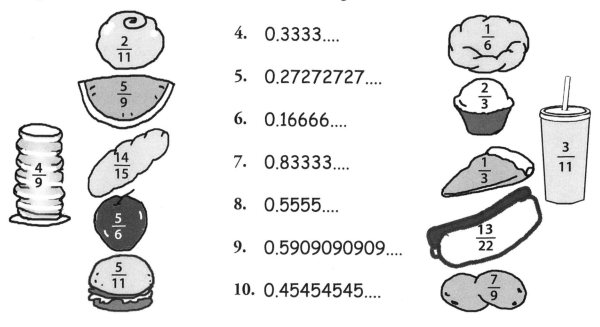

4. 0.3333....

5. 0.27272727....

6. 0.16666....

7. 0.83333....

8. 0.5555....

9. 0.5909090909....

10. 0.45454545....

$\frac{2}{11}$ $\frac{5}{9}$ $\frac{4}{9}$ $\frac{14}{15}$ $\frac{5}{6}$ $\frac{5}{11}$

$\frac{1}{6}$ $\frac{2}{3}$ $\frac{3}{11}$ $\frac{1}{3}$ $\frac{13}{22}$ $\frac{7}{9}$

Name

ON THE ROPES

The Rochester Institute of Technology, in Rochester, New York, hosts an annual tug-of-war tournament. In 2012, 1,647 students participated. The tradition is that winners get to brag and losers take a mud bath. Don't get dragged in the mud with this tug-of-war challenge; get the numbers in the right order!

For each tug-of-war contest pictured, write the four given numbers in order from smallest to largest along the rope. Do not use a calculator.

1.   4   4.2   4.12 $\sqrt{17}$

2.   2.4 $\sqrt{6}$ 3   2

3. $\sqrt{3}$ 1.5   1.7   1.74

4.   3 $\sqrt{10}$ 3.2   3.163

5.   2.6   2.65 $\sqrt{7}$ 2.61

6.   4.6   4.8 $\sqrt{23}$ 4.9

7.   5.6 $\sqrt{31}$ 5.61   5.7

8. $\sqrt{49}$ 6.6 $\sqrt{43}$ 6.5

Name

Common Core Reinforcement Activities — 8th Grade Math

THE THINGS PEOPLE THROW

Numerous sports involve throwing. It's common to watch people throwing balls. It's common to watch the throw of a hammer, shot, or discus in track and field events. But many uncommon things (some of them downright strange) are thrown in sporting competitions. Use number lines to approximate rational numbers for some of these throws.

Without using a calculator, decide which point A or B represents the location where the item will land on the number line.

1. Suzannah threw a pie in a pie-tossing contest. It landed at a number close to the value of $\sqrt{45}$. Which point (A or B) more closely represents $\sqrt{45}$?

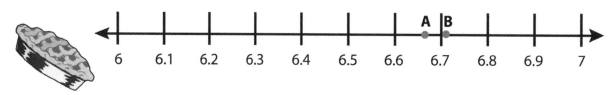

2. Marcus won a cell-phone-throwing competition. His toss landed at a number close to the value of $\sqrt{52}$. Which point (A or B) more closely represents $\sqrt{52}$?

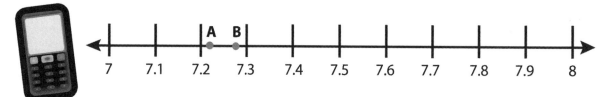

3. Allie tossed a DVD in a DVD-throwing contest. It landed at a number close to the value of $\sqrt{10}$. Which point (A or B) more closely represents $\sqrt{10}$?

4. Karim won a doughnut-tossing contest. His toss landed at a number close to the value of $\sqrt{33}$. Which point (A or B) more closely represents $\sqrt{33}$?

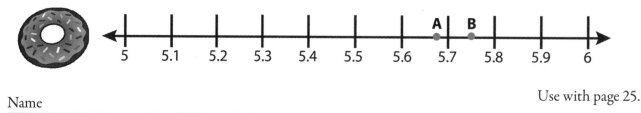

Name

Use with page 25.

Without using a calculator, decide which point, A or B, represents the location where the item will land on the number line.

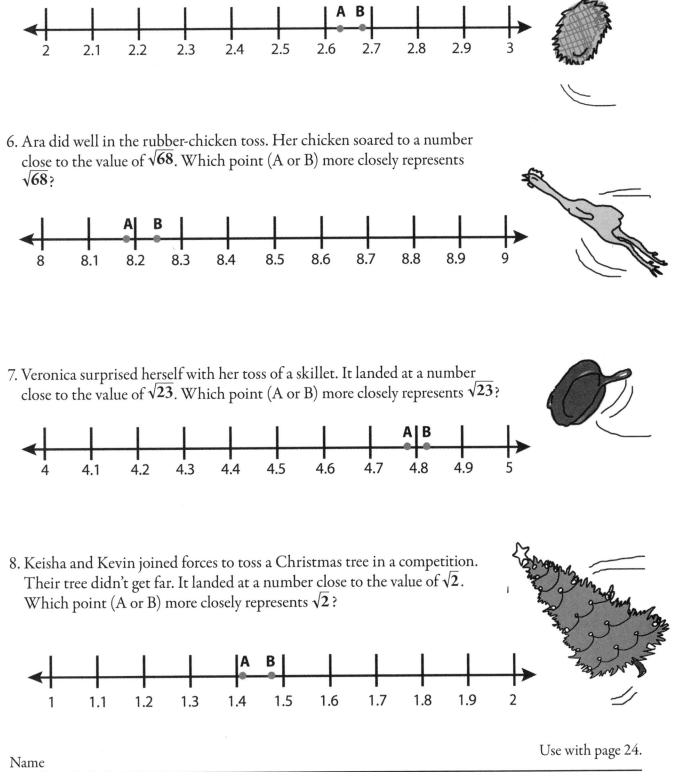

5. Joshua decided to try cow-pie tossing. (Fortunately, the cow pie was all dried out!) His toss landed at a number close to the value of $\sqrt{7}$. Which point (A or B) more closely represents $\sqrt{7}$?

6. Ara did well in the rubber-chicken toss. Her chicken soared to a number close to the value of $\sqrt{68}$. Which point (A or B) more closely represents $\sqrt{68}$?

7. Veronica surprised herself with her toss of a skillet. It landed at a number close to the value of $\sqrt{23}$. Which point (A or B) more closely represents $\sqrt{23}$?

8. Keisha and Kevin joined forces to toss a Christmas tree in a competition. Their tree didn't get far. It landed at a number close to the value of $\sqrt{2}$. Which point (A or B) more closely represents $\sqrt{2}$?

Use with page 24.

Name _____

Copyright © 2014 World Book, Inc./
Incentive Publications, Chicago, IL

AROUND THE BARRELS

The challenge in barrel racing is to guide a horse in a cloverleaf pattern around barrels in a time that is faster than that of the other riders! This takes a skilled rider and a horse in good condition.

Use your mathematical skills to race around these barrels, filling in the blanks as you go. You can set a timer to inspire speed, but don't move so fast that you make mistakes! Without using a calculator, find two numbers to fill in the blanks. They should be one-tenth apart in value and should be written to the tenths place.

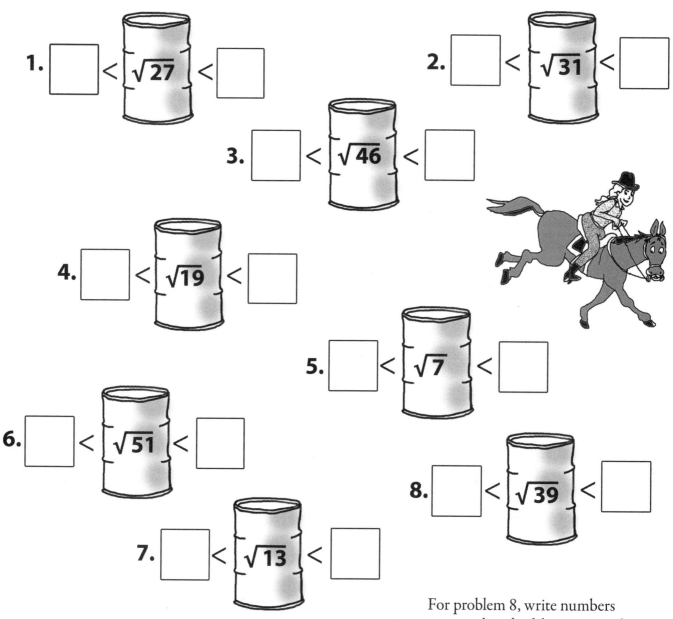

1. ☐ $< \sqrt{27} <$ ☐

2. ☐ $< \sqrt{31} <$ ☐

3. ☐ $< \sqrt{46} <$ ☐

4. ☐ $< \sqrt{19} <$ ☐

5. ☐ $< \sqrt{7} <$ ☐

6. ☐ $< \sqrt{51} <$ ☐

7. ☐ $< \sqrt{13} <$ ☐

8. ☐ $< \sqrt{39} <$ ☐

For problem 8, write numbers one-one hundredth apart in value, written to the hundredths place.

Name

EXPRESSIONS AND EQUATIONS

Grade 8

If 3x is the distance to the goal line,
how long will it take me to get there?

RIGHT ON TARGET

The dartboard shows many expressions with integer exponents. Some of them will be the right expressions to match the problems. Hit the right ones with your darts!

Find the equivalent expression on the dartboard to match each expression A-E. Draw a dart pointing to the expression. Label the dart with the letter of the problem (A, B, C, D, or E).

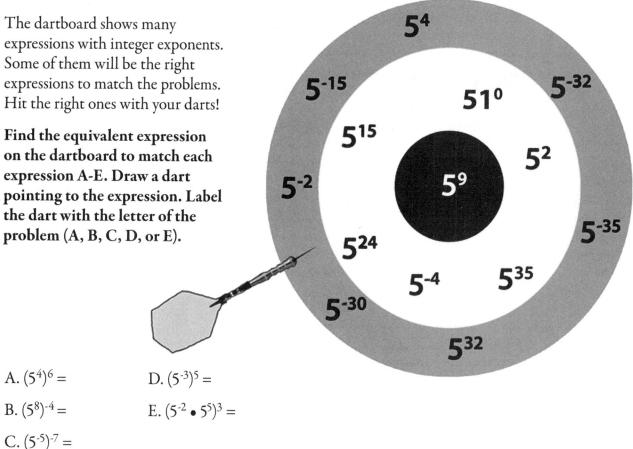

A. $(5^4)^6 =$

B. $(5^8)^{-4} =$

C. $(5^{-5})^{-7} =$

D. $(5^{-3})^5 =$

E. $(5^{-2} \cdot 5^5)^3 =$

Answer the questions.

1. If $10^3 = 5^a \cdot 2^a$, what is **a**?

2. If $(10^7)^4 = 10^b$, what is **b**?

3. If $10^3 \cdot 10^7 = 10^c$, what is **c**?

4. If $10^{-6} \cdot 10^d = 10^{30}$, what is **d**?

5. If $(15^2)^4 = 15^f$, what is **f**?

6. If $15^{-8} = 3^g \cdot 5^g$, what is **g**?

7. If $15^5 \cdot 15^{-2} = 15^k$, what is **k**?

8. If $\frac{15^9}{15^n} = 15^{11}$, what is **n**?

Name

28

EXPRESSION INSPECTION

39,013 people wearing cowboy hats gathered at a California stadium in 2012 to set a Guinness world record. One student who read about this record observed that this number, rounded, could be written as the exponential expression 200^2. This activity will help you examine and evaluate some other exponential expressions

Think about the value of each expression in problems 1-8. Mark an X in the column on the table that describes its value.

	Expression	Less than -1	Between 0 and 1	Equal to 0	Equal to 1	Greater than 1
1.	-4^5					
2.	4^{-6}					
3.	$(-4)^{-6}$					
4.	4^5					
5.	$(4^{-5})(4^{-7})$					
6.	$(3^2)(3^{-3})$					
7.	$\dfrac{1^{-2}}{1^{-4}}$					
8.	$\dfrac{5^{-4}}{5^{-4}}$					

Find the value of each expression.

9. $2^3 =$

10. $3^4 =$

11. $6^{-2} =$

12. $\left(\frac{1}{2}\right)^{-5} =$

13. $\left(\frac{1}{7}\right)^{-2} =$

14. $\left(\frac{2}{5}\right)^{-1} =$

15. $\left(\frac{1}{3}\right)^{-2} =$

16. $\left(\frac{2}{6}\right)^{-3} =$

17. $4^{-4} =$

18. $\left(\frac{7}{8}\right)^{-3} =$

Name

Common Core Reinforcement Activities — 8th Grade Math

BARBELL BALANCE

Ordinarily, the weights on both ends of a barbell are the same. Each of the barbells at Jan's gym is out of balance today because the expression at one end is not equivalent to the expression at the other end.

Evaluate each exponential expression. Then find the pairs of equivalent expressions. Cross out one expression on each barbell and write the correct one (borrowed from another barbell) on the bar between the weights.

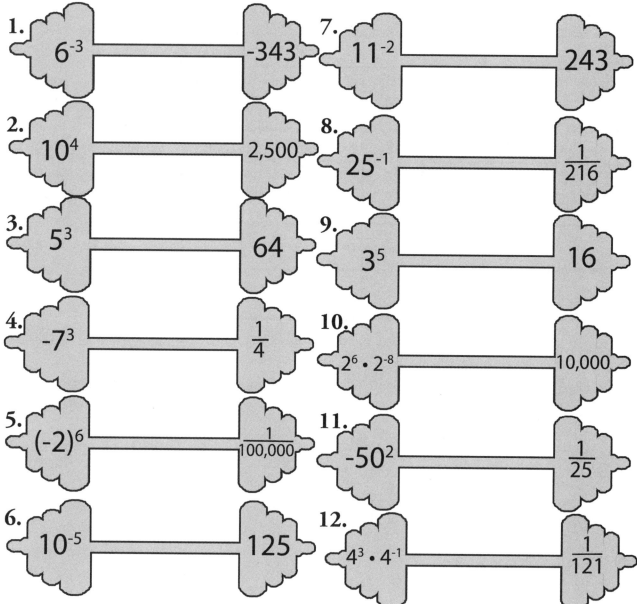

1. 6^{-3} — -343

2. 10^4 — 2,500

3. 5^3 — 64

4. -7^3 — $\frac{1}{4}$

5. $(-2)^6$ — $\frac{1}{100,000}$

6. 10^{-5} — 125

7. 11^{-2} — 243

8. 25^{-1} — $\frac{1}{216}$

9. 3^5 — 16

10. $2^6 \cdot 2^{-8}$ — 10,000

11. -50^2 — $\frac{1}{25}$

12. $4^3 \cdot 4^{-1}$ — $\frac{1}{121}$

30

Name

HOMEWORK WOES

After playing in the baseball game, Charlie finished his math homework. Maybe he was too excited about the home run he scored, or maybe he was worn out from the game. Something was wrong, because all of his problems had wrong answers.

For each problem, explain what Charlie did wrong and find the right answer. Write your answer as an exponential expression.

1. $(7^2 \cdot 4^{-10})^{-8} = (7 \cdot 4)^{160}$

2. $(6^{-8} \cdot 6^{-4}) = 6^{-4}$

3. $(5^3 \cdot 5^{-4})^2 = 5^{-24}$

4. $(4^{-4} \cdot 6^2)^{-3} = 24^{-1}$

5. $\dfrac{9^{-4}}{9^3} = 9^{-1}$

6. $\dfrac{8^{10}}{8^2} = 8^5$

7. $\left(\dfrac{4}{3}\right)^{-2} = \dfrac{16}{9}$

8. $\left(\dfrac{2}{5}\right)^{-3} = \dfrac{-125}{8}$

9. $6^{-2} = 3^6$

10. $\left(\dfrac{1}{9}\right)^{-1} = -9$

Name

Copyright © 2014 World Book, Inc./
Incentive Publications, Chicago, IL

Common Core Reinforcement Activities — 8th Grade Math

AWESOME FEATS

Two young people performed record feats showing great agility, discipline, and skill. Giulia Bencini, of Italy, was 11 when she equaled the record for the most backward flips on a balance beam in one minute. 18-year-old Jacopo Forza, also of Italy, set a world record for time spent in side splits between two objects. He "sat" (in air) suspended between two cars in a split position with his legs extended at a 180-degree angle.

Evaluate exponential expressions to solve some problems about these and other feats.

Circle the correct answer.

1. Giulia did 20 backward flips in one minute. (See opening paragraph.) Which expression most closely represents this number?

   a. $5^2 - 2^2$ b. $4^2 + 2^2$ c. $(2^2)(4^2)$

2. Jacopo held his difficult split position for 228 seconds. (See opening paragraph.) Which expression most closely represents this number?

   a. 15^2 b. $6^3 + 2^3$ c. $8^3 - 17^2$

3. Chelsea McGuffin, of Australia, set a world record for walking across tops of upright glass bottles. Which expression most closely represents the 51 bottles in her record?

   a. $3^3 + 2^5$ b. $3^2 + 6^2$ c. $(2^3)(4^2)$

4. Ho Eng Hui, of Malaysia, is the fastest person to pierce 4 coconuts with a finger. He did this in just over 12 seconds. Which expression most closely represents this time in number of minutes?

   a. $5^4 - 5$ b. -5^3 c. 5^{-5}

Circle the correct evaluation for each expression.

5. $4^{-3} =$

   $\frac{1}{64}$ -64 64 $\frac{1}{-64}$

6. $\frac{5x^4}{x} =$

   $\frac{1}{5x^4}$ $4x^3$ 54 $5x^3$

7. $3n^3 \cdot 6n^2 =$

   $9n^6$ $18n$ $18n^6$ $18n^5$

8. $\frac{a^{-8}}{a^6} =$

   a^2 a^{-14} a^2 a^{48}

9. $\left(\frac{3}{4}\right)^2 =$

   $\frac{6}{4}$ $\frac{9}{16}$ $\frac{9}{4}$ $\frac{16}{9}$

10. $-5^3 =$

   $\frac{1}{125}$ -125 $-\frac{1}{125}$ 125

Name

FOLLOW THE TRAIL

A steaming hot pizza awaits the soccer team after a game.
Team members can follow a trail of squared and cubed numbers to dinner.

**Without using a calculator, find the trail that
contains only numbers that are perfect squares or
perfect cubes. Mark the trail with your pencil.**

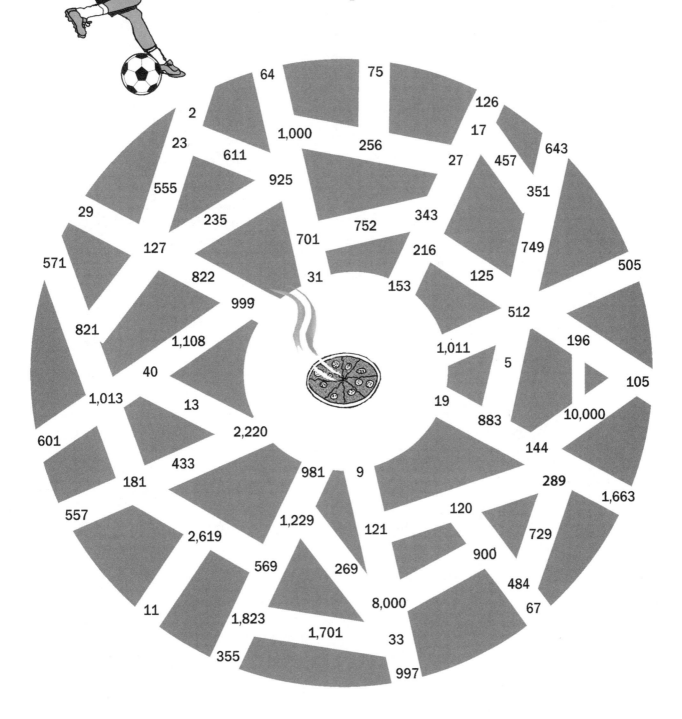

Name

Common Core Reinforcement Activities — 8th Grade Math

GOLF TRIVIA

The answers to these golf trivia questions can be found by finding numbers on the golf balls to match the expressions in the problems.

Write the letter of the problem next to the ball with the answer. Do not use a calculator.

1. The approximate number (in thousands) of golf courses in the United Sates: $\sqrt[3]{5,832}$

2. The last year that golf balls stuffed with feathers were used: $(43^2) - 1$

3. The approximate number (in millions) of people who play golf each year in the United States: $\sqrt[3]{125}$

4. The average distance (in meters) from the tee to the hole on a miniature golf course: $\sqrt{900} - \sqrt{400}$

5. The age of the youngest golfer to shoot a hole in one: $\sqrt[3]{64}$

6. The number of dimples on a regulation golf ball: $7^3 - 7$

7. The chances of making two holes in one in one round of golf are _____ in a million: $\sqrt{4,489}$

8. Jack Nicklaus has the most wins of the Masters golf tournament with this many wins: $\sqrt[3]{216}$

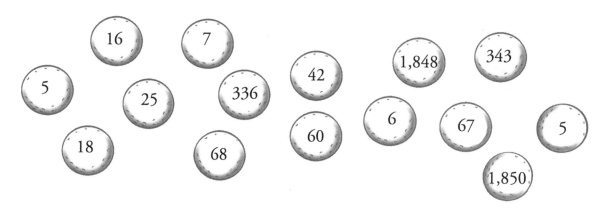

16   7   5   25   336   42   1,848   343   6   67   5   18   68   60   1,850

HEADED FOR TROUBLE

It looks as if Shania is headed for trouble. You can help her navigate Bonebreaker Boulevard. Solve this long, winding problem correctly to give her a chance of avoiding a major crash along the way. Read all the directions before you start.

As she moves along the sidewalk, Shania must ADD the value of each section to the previous section. However, when she comes to one of the seven sections with obstructions, she must leap over it and SUBTRACT the value of that section. Write the correct number in the blank section.

MASS INTRIGUE

Any sporting activity involves many items (or beings) of various masses. Sometimes the mass is a key factor in the performance of the sport. At other times, mass is just an intriguing statistic!

Write these masses in standard notation. Do not use a calculator.

1. The mass of the small airplane used for skydivers: **1.7×10^3 kilograms**

2. The mass of a skydiver getting ready to jump from the plane: **7.2×10^1 kilograms**

3. The mass of a raindrop falling near the skydiver: **5.0×10^{-6} kilograms**

4. The mass of a race horse: **5.55×10^2 kilograms**

5. The mass of the trailer that carried the horse to the race: **1.1×10^3 kilograms**

6. The mass of the flea buzzing in the horse's ear: **4.9×10^{-7} kilograms**

Write these masses in scientific notation. Do not use a calculator.

7. The mass of the nose plugs worn by a swimmer doing a moonlight swim across a channel: **0.00022 kilograms**

8. The mass of the boat (with motor and two passengers) cruising alongside the swimmer: **1,400 kilograms**

9. The mass of the moon shining over the water during the late-night swim: **73,477,000,000,000,000,000,000 kilograms**

10. The mass of a circus acrobat riding on the back of an elephant: **68.5 kilograms**

11. The weight of the circus elephant: **4,200 kilograms**

12. The weight of the feather in the elephant's headdress: **0.0066 kilograms**

Name

THE VIEW FROM SPACE

When she's on Earth, astronaut Lucinda is a fan of ballpark hot dogs. She tries them out at every ballpark she can visit. She's so skilled at tracking down these hot dogs that she insists she can even see them from outer space. When challenged by her friends about this claim, she insists, "I can find a ballpark hot dog at a distance of up to 362,500 kilometers from Earth."

If Lucinda is not exaggerating, from which of these distances (in kilometers) could she see the hot dog? (Circle them.)

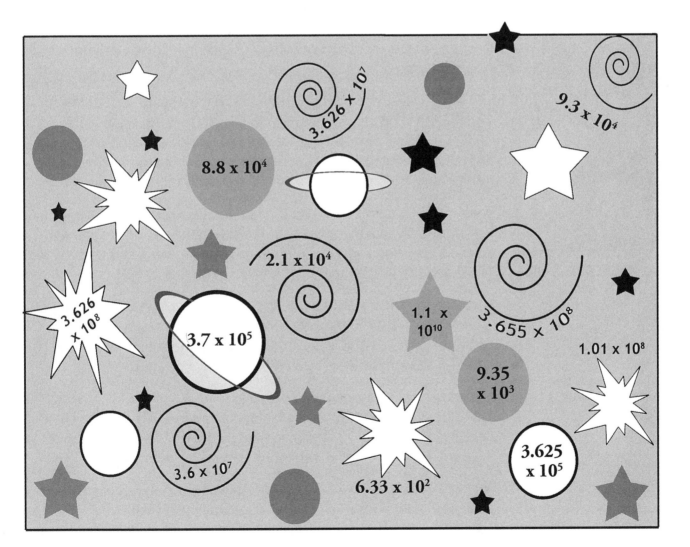

3.626×10^7

9.3×10^4

8.8×10^4

2.1×10^4

1.1×10^{10}

3.655×10^8

1.01×10^8

3.626×10^8

3.7×10^5

9.35×10^3

3.6×10^7

6.33×10^2

3.625×10^5

Name _____

Common Core Reinforcement Activities — 8th Grade Math

OUT-OF-THIS-WORLD NUMBERS

Because the pull of gravity is less strong on the moon than on Earth, we can watch videos of astronauts bouncing on the moon as if they were on trampolines. Imagine how easy it would be to clear hurdles in a moon race! Of course, before they can enjoy the jumping, the astronauts must first reach the moon. According to NASA (National Aeronautics and Space Administration), Earth's moon is approximately 360,000 kilometers from Earth at its closest point. At the point where it is farthest from Earth, the moon is approximately 405,000 kilometers away.

Use your understanding of scientific notation to solve these problems about some large numbers in space.

Mercury
Venus
Earth
and
Mars

1. Write and solve an equation using scientific notation to show the difference between the two distances from Earth in the moon's orbit described in the paragraph above. Write the answer in scientific notation.

2. Assume that a space ship travels to the moon when it is at a spot in its orbit about 3.45×10^5 kilometers from Earth. If it travels at a rate of 9.0×10^3 kilometers per hour, could its passengers reach the moon in 40 hours or less?

3. The NASA website tells visitors that, to travel in the fastest spaceship from Earth to the closest star beyond our sun, the trip would take 7.0×10^4 years. Write this number in standard notation. If it were possible to travel there and you started your trip at age 10, how many more years would you have to live to make this trip one way?

4. The average distance between the sun and Earth is 92,960,000 miles. Venus is 25,720,000 miles closer to the sun than Earth. Write and solve an equation using scientific notation to estimate the distance between Venus and the sun. Write the answer in scientific notation.

5. A light year is the distance in meters that light travels in a year. The speed of light is 3×10^8 meters per second. There are about 3.15×10^7 seconds in a year. What is the approximate distance (in meters) that light travels in a year? Write the answer in scientific notation.

6. Mercury, the smallest planet in the solar system, has a mass of about 3.3×10^{23} kilograms. Jupiter, the largest planet in Earth's solar system, has a mass of 1.9×10^{27} kilograms. Would it be true to say that Jupiter's mass is over 1,000 times greater than the mass of Mercury?

7. Former planet Pluto (now classified as a dwarf planet) has a mass of 1.5×10^{22} kilograms. The mass of some golf balls is about 5.0×10^{-3} kilograms. How many golf balls would it take to equal the weight of Pluto? Write the answer in scientific notation.

Name

WATERY QUESTIONS

Sam spends hours in his pool, training for swimming competitions. He also spends some time keeping the pool full and fishing out bugs!

Without using a calculator, solve the scientific notation problems. Write all answers in scientific notation.

1. An Olympic-sized swimming pool holds a volume of 2.5×10^6 liters of water. Start with an empty pool, and assume you could fill it at a rate of 2.0×10^5 liters per hour. How many hours would it take to fill the pool? Write and solve an equation in scientific notation.

2. Sam's backyard pool holds 1.82×10^5 liters of water. He's always dreamed of filling it with cherry soda. (He thinks this would inspire him to practice swimming more often.) His can of cherry soda contains 3.5×10^{-1} liters. How many of these cans of cherry soda would he need to fill his empty pool? Write and solve an equation in scientific notation.

It's time to roll!

3. After 2,000 liters of water in Sam's pool evaporated, the mass of the water in the pool was 1.8×10^5 kilograms. The small pillbugs that litter the pool bottom each have a mass of about 3.0×10^{-5} kilograms. How many pillbugs would it take to equal the weight of the remaining water? Write and solve an equation in scientific notation.

4. $(6.2 \times 10^2)\ (5.0 \times 10^{-6}) =$

5. $(50)\ (1 \times 10^8) =$

6. $(5.5)\ (4 \times 10^3) =$

7. $\dfrac{5.4 \times 10^{-4}}{8 \times 10^{-6}} =$

8. $\dfrac{7 \times 10^3}{7 \times 10^5} =$

9. $\dfrac{12 \times 10^{-4}}{6 \times 10^{-7}} =$

10. $\dfrac{(3.9 \times 10^2)\ (2.0 \times 10^{-6})}{3.0 \times 10^2} =$

11. $\dfrac{(4.5 \times 10^2)\ (8.0 \times 10^3)}{1.2 \times 10^8} =$

12. $\dfrac{(9.5 \times 10^{-5})\ (4.0 \times 10^9)}{9.5 \times 10^{-2}} =$

Name

Common Core Reinforcement Activities — 7th Grade Math

FACING THE GRID

Charlie faces a grid of numbers at every football practice.
At home, he faces a grid for graphing equations.
Help him out with these graphs!

Follow the instructions in each problem.

1. Graph the equation: **y = 1.5x**

   Which of the following statements are
   true? (Circle all that apply.)

   a. The slope of the line is $\frac{3}{2}$.

   b. A change of 2 units in **x** results in
      a change of 3 units in **y**.

   c. The equation represents a proportional
      relationship.

   d. A change of 3 units in **x** results in
      a change of 4.5 units in **y**.

2. Graph the equation: $y = \frac{4}{3x}$
   Which of the following statements are
   true? (Select all that apply.)

   a. The unit rate of change of **y** with
      respect to **x** is $\frac{4}{3}$.

   b. The equation represents a proportional
      relationship.

   c. A change of 3 units in **x** results in
      a change of 4 units in **y**.

   d. The slope of the line is $\frac{4}{3}$.

Name

Use with page 41.

Follow the instructions in each problem.

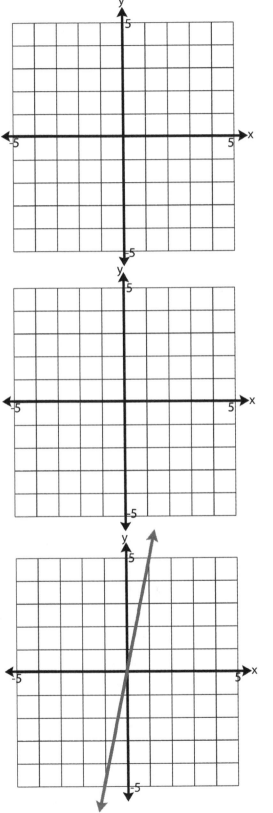

3. Graph the line that represents a proportional relationship between **a** and **b**, such that an increase of one unit in **a** corresponds to an increase of two units in **b**.

   What is the unit rate of change?

4. Graph the line that represents a proportional relationship between **x** and **y** with a unit rate of change of $\frac{5}{3}$ units in y.

   Give the equation of the line in y = kx form.

5. Is the unit rate of change of **y** with respect to **x** less or more in the graph than the unit change of rate in the equation **y = 5x**?

   Circle one answer.

   a. less

   b. more

   c. same

Use with page 40.

Name

Common Core Reinforcement Activities — 8th Grade Math

EATS, RATES, AND SALES

Solve some sports problems that involve food, speed, and good deals. They'll also require you to understand proportions!

Answer the question in each problem.

1. Rhonda is a speed skater. She eats the same number of calories every day while in training. The table shows her cumulative caloric intake for 3 days.

Day	1	2	3
Calories	4,000	8,000	12,000

Which of the following equations, if any, represents someone with a caloric intake greater than Rhonda's (**c** represents calories and **d** represents a day)?

a. c = 3,999d   c. c = 2,500d

b. c = 3,100d   d. c = 4,100d

2. John rowed his boat at a steady rate. After 2 hours, he had gone 5.3 miles. Jake rowed his boat at a rate given by the equation **d = 2.55t** (**t** in hours).

Which is correct?

a. John rowed faster.

b. Jake rowed faster.

c. John and Jake rowed at the same rate.

3. Two sporting goods stores are having competing sales. Al's Sporting Goods has a sale graphed below. In this graph, **y** represents the new sale price and **x** represents the original price.

Jerry's Sporting Goods has a sale represented by the equation **s = 0.29p**. (s = sale price; p = original price)

Which sale is better?

a. Al's

b. Jerry's

c. There is no difference.

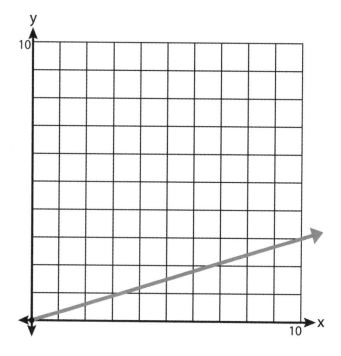

Name

SLOPE-STYLE MATH

Snowboarders and skiers are not the only ones who face challenging slopes! Take on these slopes. It's not hard if you've come prepared.

Use the graphs to solve the problems. Follow the directions for each one.

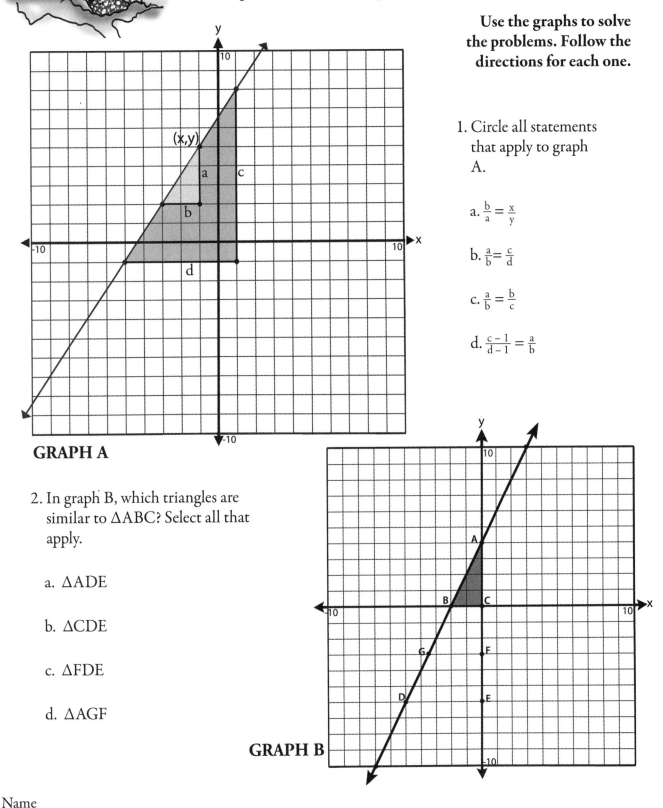

1. Circle all statements that apply to graph A.

   a. $\frac{b}{a} = \frac{x}{y}$

   b. $\frac{a}{b} = \frac{c}{d}$

   c. $\frac{a}{b} = \frac{b}{c}$

   d. $\frac{c-1}{d-1} = \frac{a}{b}$

GRAPH A

2. In graph B, which triangles are similar to $\triangle ABC$? Select all that apply.

   a. $\triangle ADE$

   b. $\triangle CDE$

   c. $\triangle FDE$

   d. $\triangle AGF$

GRAPH B

Name

Common Core Reinforcement Activities — 8th Grade Math

Use the graphs to solve the problems. Follow the directions for each one.

3.

A. Use any of the points on the line in graph C to help complete the equation

$$\frac{y+3}{x} = \underline{\hspace{2cm}}$$

B. Write the equation of the line in the form **y = mx + b.**

4.

Which triangles in graph D are similar to △ABC?

Select all that apply.

a. △AEF

b. △ADG

c. △BEF

d. △DCF

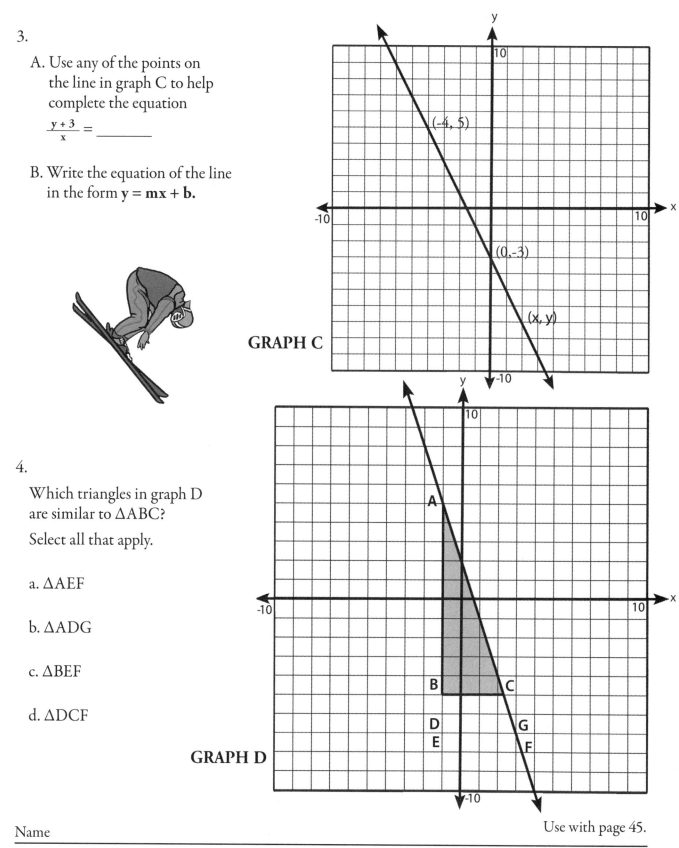

GRAPH C

GRAPH D

Name

Use with page 45.

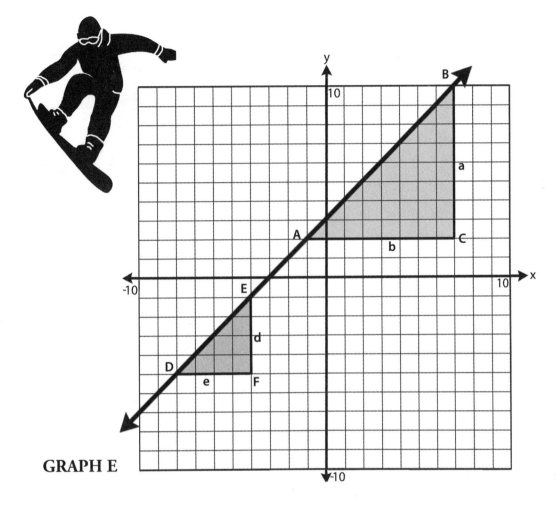

GRAPH E

5.

The following is a proof that △ABC and △DEF on graph E are similar and hence $\frac{a}{b} = \frac{d}{e}$. Give the reason for each step (A - E) in the proof.

A. ∠EFD = ∠BCA

B. ∠DEF = ∠ABC

C. ∠EDF = ∠BAC

D. △DEF is similar to △ABC

E. $\frac{a}{b} = \frac{d}{e}$

6.
TRUE OR FALSE?
You have just shown that the slope of a line is constant.

Name

Use with page 44.

GOOD CATCHES

The fishing is good today. Every net has at least one catch! Look for linear equations that belong in the different nets.

A. Decide whether each equation has one solution, no solution, or infinitely many solutions. Simplify the equation to show which is the case.

B. Write the problem number in the correct fishing net to show where each equation lands in relation to the number of solutions.

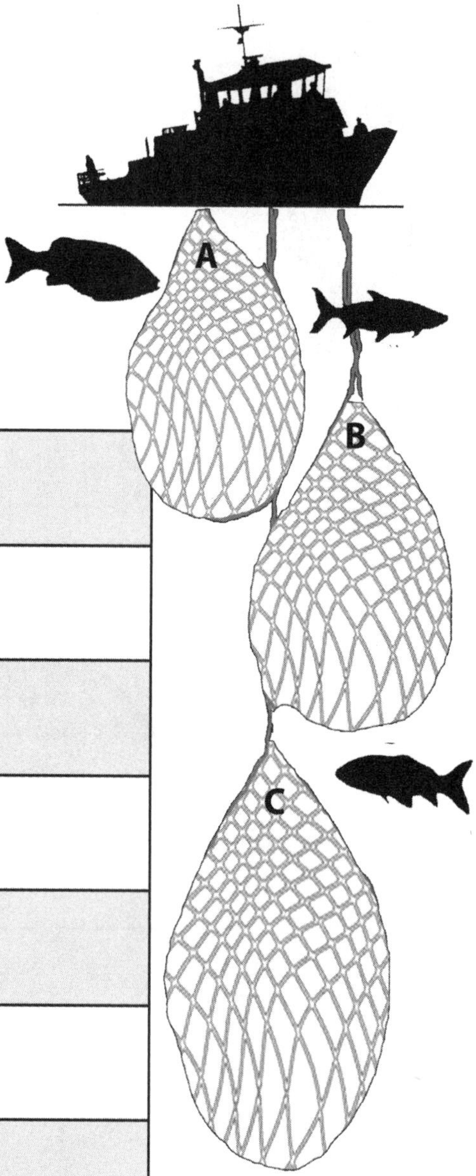

1.	$5b = -4b + 9b$
2.	$5 + 3(x + 2) = 6x + 2$
3.	$20x - 10 - 5x = -10 + 15x$
4.	$-5 + 4(x + 4) = x + 3(x + 4)$
5.	$-x = -x - 8$
6.	$3(x + 8) - 24 = 9 - 6x$
7.	$10d - 11 = 10d + 4$
8.	$-4b - 2 = -2 - 4b$
9.	$-4x - 4 = 4x$
10.	$-8x + 7x = -x$

A. One solution

B. No solutions

C. Infinitely many solutions

Name

Use with page 47.

Continue making good catches by simplifying each equation. Then circle the correct answer for each question.

11. Which of the following choices of **n** will result in a linear equation with no solutions?

    -n = -n – 6

    a. any number

    b. 6

    c. any negative number

    d. any number except -6

    e. 8

12. Which linear equation has no solutions?

    a. 10x – 7 = x

    b. 10x + 6 = 10x – 5

    c. 10x – 3(x + 6) = 2x + 7

13. Which value of **b** will form a linear equation with no solutions?

    10a – 7 = 10a + b

    a. any number

    b. any negative number

    c. any number except -7

14. Which numbers for the blanks will form a linear equation with no solutions?

    30x + 20 = _____ x + _____

    a. 30, 20

    b. 20, 30

    c. -10, 20

    d. 30, 19

15. Which number for the blank will form a linear equation with no solutions?

    8(x – 3) + 2 = 8x + _____

    a. any number

    b. any negative number

    c. any number except -22

16. Which numbers for the blanks will form a linear equation with infinitely many solutions?

    6x + 10 = 4 + _____ x + _____

    a. 6, 10

    b. 6, 6

    c. -6, 4

    d. 10, 6

Use with page 46.

Name

Common Core Reinforcement Activities — 8th Grade Math

EQUATIONS ON ICE

The pucks have solutions, but you'll have to do the math to find which one fits each equation

Solve the equations to find the hockey facts. Write a solution from one of the hockey pucks.

1. A 2008 international ice hockey match between the Slovakian and Bulgarian women's teams resulted in the highest score for a match in international history. Slovakia scored 82 points. Solve the equation for **b** to find Bulgaria's score.

$$-8b + 12 = \frac{-18b + 24}{2}$$

2. The women's ice hockey team of Canada has won a record number of gold medals in the Winter Olympics, with the most recent win in 2014. Solve the equation for **g** to find the number of gold medals.

$$4(3.5 + g) = 2g + 22$$

3. Two countries, Russia (formerly included in the USSR) and Canada, are tied for the number of gold medals in men's ice hockey at the Winter Olympics. Solve the equation for **m** to find the number of gold medals each has earned.

$$6(2m + 4) - m = 14m$$

4. Ralph DeLeo, of the United States, holds the record for scoring the most consecutive goals in an ice hockey match. This feat took place in a college game in 1953. Solve the equation for **c** to find the number of consecutive goals he scored.

$$-3x - 19 + 10x - 21 = x + 12 + x + -2$$

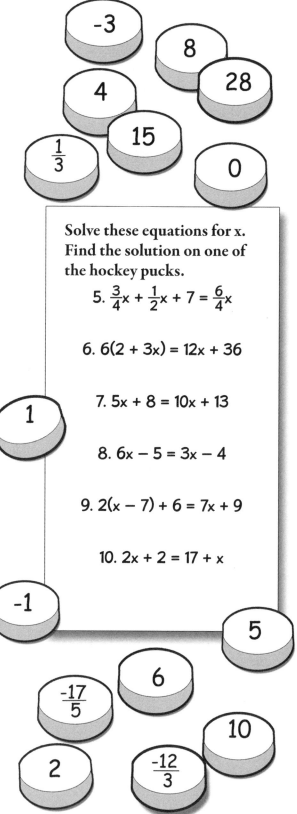

Solve these equations for x. Find the solution on one of the hockey pucks.

5. $\frac{3}{4}x + \frac{1}{2}x + 7 = \frac{6}{4}x$

6. $6(2 + 3x) = 12x + 36$

7. $5x + 8 = 10x + 13$

8. $6x - 5 = 3x - 4$

9. $2(x - 7) + 6 = 7x + 9$

10. $2x + 2 = 17 + x$

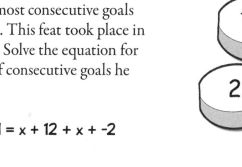

Name

THE SPLATTERED HOMEWORK

Oh, oh! Malika should not have left her homework outdoors during the paintball competition. She worked hard on those equations, but now some of her good work is impossible to read.

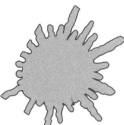

Assume that Malika's solutions are correct. Replace the number or operational symbol in each equation that is obscured by paint splatter.

A. $2(2x - 5) + \text{\_\_} = -10$ $x = -5$

B. $4x + x \text{\_\_} 7 = x + 9$ $x = \frac{1}{2}$

C. $\text{\_\_} = 6x + 3 - 11$ $x = 3$

D. $5 - 2x + 8 = -3x + \text{\_\_}$ $x = -7$

E. $3x(1 + 2) + \text{\_\_} = -18$ $x = -1$

F. $-120 \text{\_\_} 12x + 9 = 9$ $x = 10$

G. $\text{\_\_}x + (10x - 4) = -1$ $x = \frac{1}{10}$

Name

Common Core Reinforcement Activities — 8th Grade Math

BY THE NUMBERS

Many sporting events are won or lost by numbers—numbers of minutes, seconds, miles, balls hit into holes, or other things counted. Running events need numbers to measure distances and times.

Write and solve an equation to find a number to answer each of these sports questions.

1. In a race, 4 sprinters finish in times that are consecutive whole even number minutes. The sum of the times is 500. What is the race time of the fourth sprinter to cross the finish line?

2. In a race, 5 hurdlers finish in times that are consecutive whole odd number minutes. The sum of the times is 395. What is the race time of the fourth runner to cross the finish line?

3. In a race, 5 runners finish in times that are consecutive whole odd number minutes. The sum of the times is 475. What is the race time of the fifth runner to cross the finish line?

4. In a race, 6 runners finish in times that are consecutive whole odd number minutes. The sum of the times is 852. What is the race time of the third runner to cross the finish line?

These equations are already solved. Find the mixture of numbers and variables (the equation) that led to each solution!

5. The solution is x = 2.
   Which is the equation?

   a. $\frac{1}{3}x = 6$

   b. $\frac{4x}{2} = -4 + 4x$

   c. $\frac{1}{4}x = \frac{1}{2}$

   d. $\frac{2}{1}x - 6 = 0$

6. The solution is x = 5.
   Which is the equation?

   a. $x - 5 + 4x = -20$

   b. $x + 7 - 4x = -8$

   c. $2(x + 9) = x + 3$

   d. $\frac{5x}{3} + x = 8x - 10$

7. The solution is x = $-\frac{1}{2}$.
   Which is the equation?

   a. $-12x - 9 + 8x = 1$

   b. $10(x + 3) = 6x$

   c. $-12x + 9 + 8x = 11$

   d. $x(7 + 5) - 4x = 0$

8. The solution is x = -10.
   Which is the equation?

   a. $4(x + 4) - x = 6x$

   b. $5(6x + 12) = 30x$

   c. $10 - 3x + 5 = -4x + 5$

   d. $\frac{5x}{10} = -x - 5$

Name

TENNIS TROUBLES

Spenser is having some trouble with his tennis swing. He's hitting most of his strokes into the net.

Solve the puzzle in the net by finding the value of the variables. Notice the operational signs between tennis balls in each row and each column. Write the value of each variable below the puzzle.

a = _____   b = _____   c = _____   d = _____   e = _____

AGE-OLD PROBLEMS

Mathematics students have been solving age problems for ages! Your experience with writing and solving equations will come in handy for finding ages in the future or past for one or more people.

Write and solve an equation to answer each age question.

1. J.R. is twice as old as T.R. The sum of their ages is five times T.R.'s age less 48. How old is T.R.?

2. Louisa is 5 years less than three times Brie's age. The sum of their ages is 43. How old is Louisa?

3. The coach, Sara, is four times the age of each of the players on her team. In 10 years, Sara will be twice as old as these players. How old are these players now?

4. Josh is half the age of his teammate, Juniper. In two years the sum of their ages will be 28. How old is Juniper?

5. 16 years from now, Laura, the catcher on a softball team, will be three times as old as she is today. What is her current age?

6. 5 years ago, Katelyn was half of the age she will be in 8 years. How old is she now?

7. Jose and Abby, brother and sister, both love to throw, catch, and hit balls. 4 years from now, Jose will be twice Abby's age at that time. The sum of their ages in 4 years will be 30. How old are they now?

8. In 21 years, pitcher Todd will be four times older than he is today. What is his age today?

9. Savannah is 4 years older than Mariah. In 13 years, the sum of their ages will be 68. How old are they now?

10. Jay is twice as old as May. Ray is 6 years older than May. The sum of their ages is 34. How old is Ray?

Name

ONE, MANY, OR NONE?

Isabel's wondering which route, if any, will take her to Emerald Lake. There could be many, but probably not infinitely many. When you see a system of linear equations, there may be one possible solution or no solutions. Or, unlike Isabel's problem about the routes to Emerald Lake, there may be infinitely many solutions!

Which way do I go?

How many solutions exist for the solution of each system shown? Circle one answer.

1. $x + y = 8$
$y = x + 6$
a. one solution
b. infinitely many solutions
c. no solutions

2. $x + y = 4$
$2x = 6 - 2y$
a. one solution
b. infinitely many solutions
c. no solutions

3. $x + y = 6$
$3x + 3y = 3$
a. one solution
b. infinitely many solutions
c. no solutions

4. $x - 2y = 2$
$2x = 4y + 4$
a. one solution
b. infinitely many solutions
c. no solutions

Circle one answer for each question.

5. Which of the following choices of **a** will result in a system of linear equations with no solutions?
$6x - 2y = 5$
$3x - y = a$
a. any number
b. $\frac{5}{2}$
c. any number except $\frac{5}{2}$
d. any number except 14

6. Which of the following choices of **a** will result in a system of linear equations with infinitely many solutions?
$6x - 2y = 5$
$3x - y = a$
a. any number
b. $\frac{5}{2}$
c. any number except $\frac{5}{2}$
d. any number except 14

7. Which of the following choices of **a** will result in a system of linear equations with infinitely many solutions?
$-x + 3y = -4$
$x - 3y = a$
a. any number
b. any number except 4
c. 4
d. any number except -3

Name

Common Core Reinforcement Activities — 8th Grade Math

PROCEED WITH CAUTION

In the spirit of daredevil undertakings, some people have taken to throwing and catching running chainsaws. Australians Chayne Hultgren threw a running chainsaw 13 feet (4 m) and Gordo Gamsby caught it to set a record for the farthest distance thrown and caught. People who undertake such adventures must proceed with caution. Don't try this at home (or anywhere else)!

Proceed with caution as you solve linear equations. There may be unexpected outcomes. There may be no solution or many solutions.

1. You are solving a system of linear equations in two variables and you find there are no solutions. Which is a possible graph of the system? Circle all that apply.

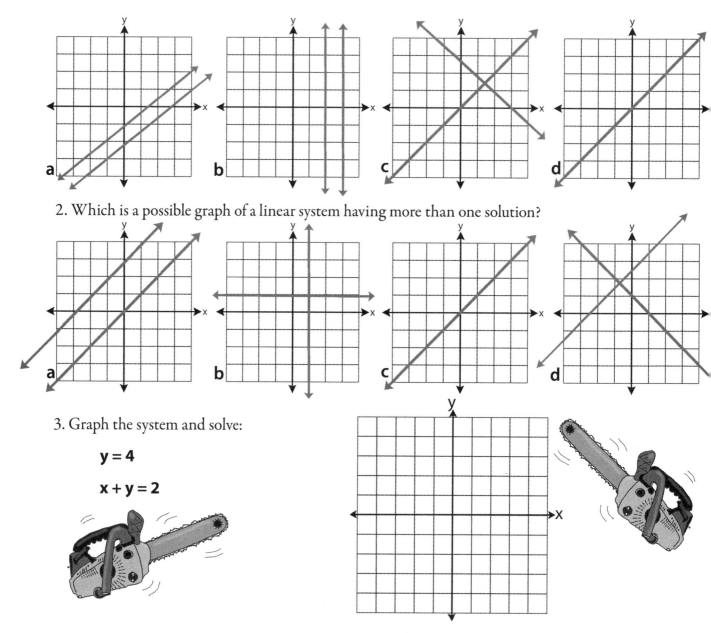

2. Which is a possible graph of a linear system having more than one solution?

3. Graph the system and solve:

$$y = 4$$

$$x + y = 2$$

As if firewalking and bungee jumping, each by themselves, were not dangerous enough, some people combine the two in another daredevil activity. Yoni Roch, of France, doubled the danger by bungee jumping from a record height of 65.09 meters (123 ft) into water while in a suit that was on fire.

Proceed with caution as you solve linear equations. There may be unexpected outcomes. There may be no solution or many solutions.

4. When trying to solve the system

$$x + y = 5$$
$$5x + 5y = 25$$

you use correct steps that lead to the expression $0 = 0$.

Which statement is true?

a. $x = 0, y = 0$

b. The system has one solution.

c. The system has no solutions.

d. The system has infinitely many solutions.

5. When trying to solve the system

$$3x + 2y = 0$$
$$-3x + y = 6$$

you use correct steps that lead to the expression $3y = 6$.

Which statement is true?

a. $y = -2; x = \frac{4}{3}$

b. $y = 2; x = -\frac{4}{3}$

c. The system has infinitely many solutions.

d. The system has no solutions.

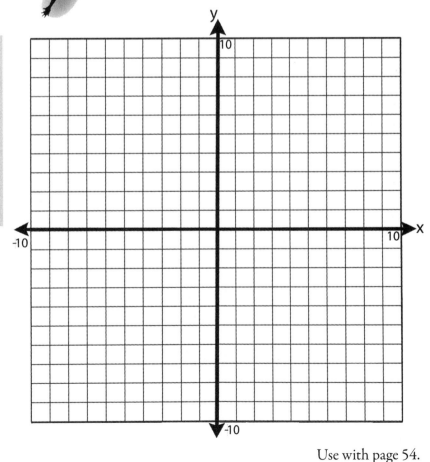

6. Fill in the blanks for the coefficients of **x** and **y** such that the system has infinitely many solutions.

$$8x + 4y = 16$$

☐ x + ☐ y = 4

7. Use the blank grid on the right to graph the system.

$$y = x + 4$$
$$y = -x + 10$$

Solve the system:

x =

y =

Use with page 54.

Name

ON THE BOARD

Blindfold chess is a form of the game where players conduct the game mentally. They don't actually move pieces or see them, but communicate moves with a system of mathematical notations. Miguel Najdorf, a Polish-born Argentinian, simultaneously played 45 games of chess. In about $23\frac{1}{2}$ hours, he won 39 of the games.

Solve each system of equations for x and y.

Hold your horses, I'm thinking!

1. Solve for x and y.

$5x + 3y = 17$
$x + 3y = 1$

2. Solve for x and y.

$3x - 5y = 19$
$x + 2x - 4y = 16$

3. Solve for x and y using elimination.

$x + 4y = 6$
$x - 2y = 18$

4. Solve for x and y using elimination.

$8x - 1 = 3y$
$8x + 1 = 9y$

5. Solve for x and y using substitution.

$y = 2x$
$7x - y = 35$

6. Solve for x and y.

$4x - 2y = -14$
$4x - 5y = -32$

7. Solve for x and y.

$6x + 12y = 7$
$8x - 15y = -1$

8. Solve for x and y.

$10x + 4y = 58$
$13x - 4y = 57$

9. Solve for x and y.

$3x + 10 = 5y$
$7x + 20 = -5y$

10. Solve for x and y.

$3x + 5y = 9$
$3x - y = -9$

Name

A MATTER OF AGE

Most sports attract athletes of many ages. Taekwondo, a Korean martial art, is no exception. According to the British Branch of the World Taekwondo Federation, about 30,000,000 people of many ages around the world practice taekwondo. Children start this sport at very young ages, and interest in martial arts is growing fast among senior citizens.

Write and solve a system of linear equations to solve each of these age problems.

1. Two friends practice taekwondo in the same class. The age of the older friend is three times that of the younger. The sum of their ages is eight more than twice the age of the younger. Find the ages.

2. Maxie and Julia are sisters who practice taekwondo together. The sum of their ages is 18. In 5 years, Julia, the older sister, will be 7 years older than Maxie is now. What are their ages now?

3. Maxwell Jr. learned taekwondo from his dad, Maxwell. The sum of their ages is 50. In 5 years, the father will be 3 times as old as his son will be then. What are their ages now?

4. Alison is the mother and coach of one of the students, Nelson. In 8 years, Alison will be twice as old as her son will be then. 3 years ago, Alison was 3 times as old as Nelson was then. What are their ages now?

5. April and May are teammates. The sum of their ages now is 30. 10 years from now, April, the older teammate, will be 4 years more than twice May's age now. What are their ages now?

6. Larry and Moe are teammates. Larry is 10 years older than Moe. In 10 years, Larry's age will be 5 times Moe's age now. What are their ages now?

7. A taekwondo instructor is 20 years older than his youngest student. In eight years, the instructor's age will be 5 years more than twice the student's age then. What are their ages now?

Name

SURFING NOSTALGIA

Surfers and friends of surfers turn the clock back to 1966 to enjoy an old surfing movie and step into some problems.

Write and solve a system of linear equations to solve each problem.

1. A group of surfing fans went to the movie theater to see a special showing of *The Endless Summer,* a surfing classic. Tickets were $3.50 for students from the local high school and $5.00 for anyone else. The group paid a total of $78.00 for tickets. If there were two more people not from the high school than from the high school, how many of each kind of customer went to the movie?

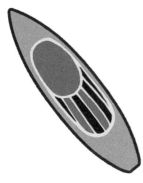

2. The air conditioner at the theater broke down halfway through the movie. The theater called in an electrician right away. The electrician worked 3 hours and her assistant worked for 5 hours. The charge was $275. If each of them had worked 2 hours longer, the bill would have been $425. Use a system of linear equations to find the hourly rates of pay for the electrician and her helper.

3. At the theater snack bar, a caramel apple costs a total of $6.75. If a customer buys two caramel apples and two turtles at the same time, the cost is $14. Using a system of linear equations, is it possible to find a unique value for a caramel apple and a unique value for a turtle? Circle one answer.

   a. Yes, $3.75 for a caramel apple and $3.00 for a turtle.

   b. Yes, $3.00 for a caramel apple and $3.75 for a turtle.

   c. No, the system has infinite solutions.

   d. No, the system has no solution.

Solve each system for x and y.

4. $9 = 8x - 5y$

   $10 + 7y = 6x$

   x =

   y =

5. $y = 4x - 1$

   $6x + y = 79$

   x =

   y =

Name

FUNCTIONS

Grade 8

Maybe I could function better if I tied my shoelaces?

QUESTIONS OF FUNCTION

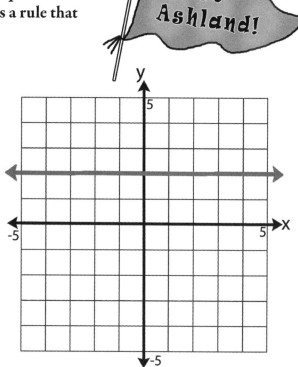

Don't forget this function fact as you answer the questions on this page and the next (page 61): A function is a rule that assigns exactly one output to each input.

Solve the problems.

1. Every person who buys a ticket to the Ashland High School Homecoming football game gets 2 raffle tickets. Brianna buys 1 ticket to the game and gets 2 raffle tickets. Twins Jay and Jamie each buy 1 ticket. They get a total of 4 raffle tickets. The Ruiz family buys 6 tickets. They get a total of 12 raffle tickets.

   Does this situation represent a function? Explain your answer.

2. In the formula $C = \pi D$, is C a function of D?

3. Could the following coordinate pairs represent a function?

   (1, -1)   (3, 2)   (4, 6)   (1, 0)

4. In the formula $A = s^2$, is A a function of s?

5. Could the following table represent a function?

x	y
2	4
3	9
4	6
4	7

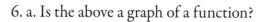

6. a. Is the above a graph of a function?

   b. What is its equation?

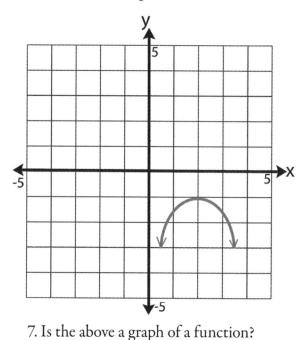

7. Is the above a graph of a function?

Don't forget this function fact as you continue to answer these questions of function:
A function is a rule that assigns exactly one output to each input.

8. Could the following table represent a function?

x	1	2	3	4	5	6
y	2	3	4	5	6	7

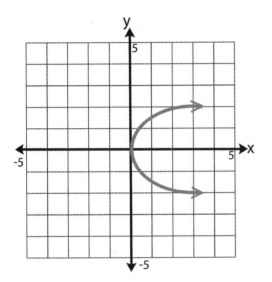

9. Is the above a graph of a function?

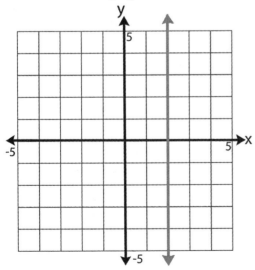

10. a. Is the above a graph of a function?

   b. What is its equation?

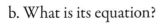

11. The bottled water machine outside the locker room is unpredictable. Daniel puts in 1 dollar and gets 2 bottles of water. Jamal puts in 2 dollars and gets 2 bottles of water. Al puts in 1 dollar and gets 1 bottle of water.

   Does this situation represent a function? Explain your answer.

12. Could the following coordinate pairs represent a function?

   (1, 0)   (2, 1)   (3, 1)   (4, 1)   (4.5, 5)

13. Does $x = 3$ represent y as a function of x?

14. Is the equation $y = -3x^2 + 2$ a function?

15. Is $f(x) = x + 3$ a function?

16. Does the following table represent a function?

x	y
0	0
1	1
2	2
3	3
4	5

Use with page 60.

Name

Common Core Reinforcement Activities — 8th Grade Math

THE CURVED PATH

A parabola is somewhat like the path a ball follows when it is thrown or hit high into the air and falls back down. If nothing interferes with the movement of the ball, it can form a curved, symmetrical path.

Explore, graph, and solve the parabola problems on this page and the next page (page 63).

1. Create a table with at least four points for the function

   $y = \frac{1}{2}x + 1.$

2. Create a graph of a function from the points shown on the table.

   Fill in the curve as smoothly as you can.

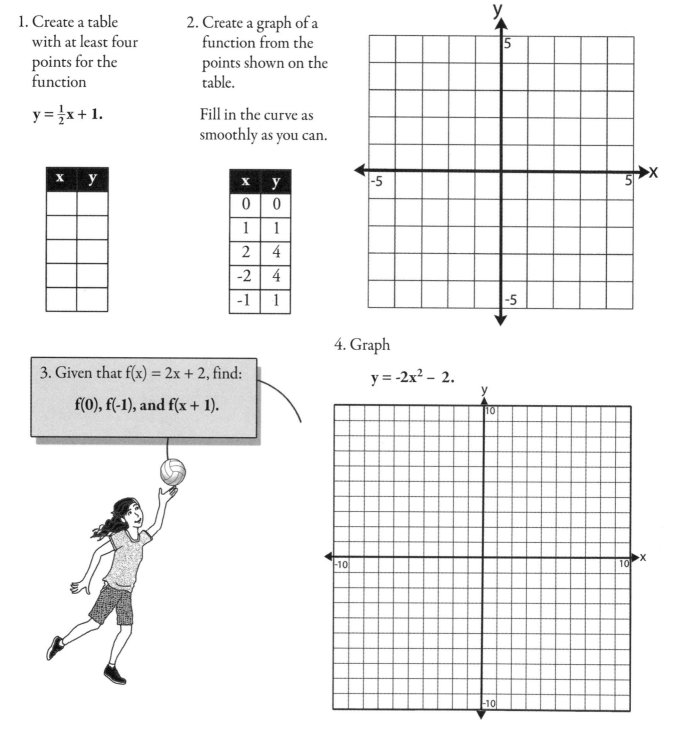

x	y

x	y
0	0
1	1
2	4
-2	4
-1	1

3. Given that f(x) = 2x + 2, find:

   f(0), f(-1), and f(x + 1).

4. Graph

   $y = -2x^2 - 2.$

THE CURVED PATH, continued

Continue exploring, graphing, and solving the parabola problems.

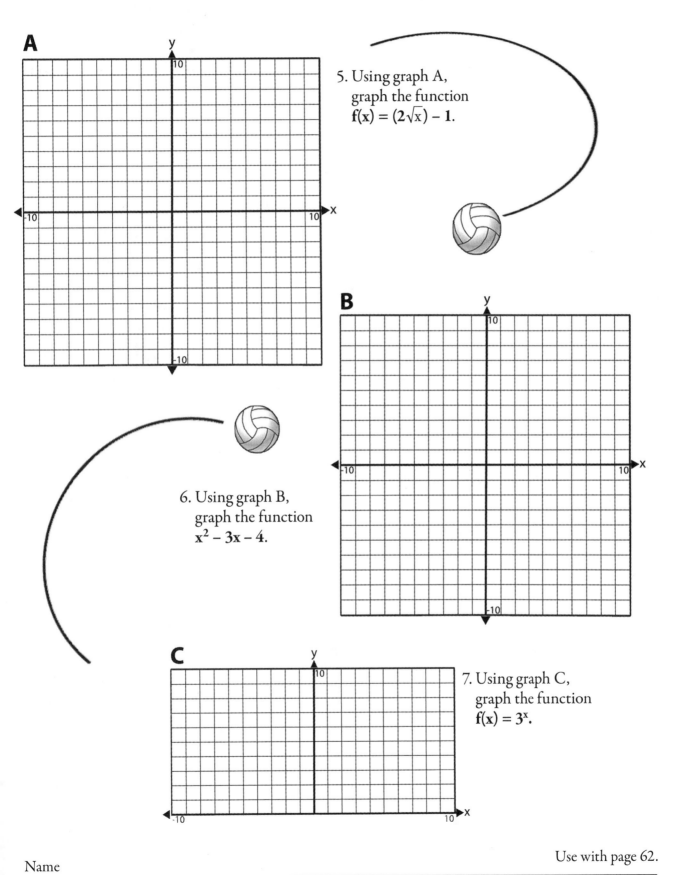

A

5. Using graph A,
   graph the function
   $f(x) = (2\sqrt{x}) - 1$.

6. Using graph B,
   graph the function
   $x^2 - 3x - 4$.

B

C

7. Using graph C,
   graph the function
   $f(x) = 3^x$.

Use with page 62.

Name

Common Core Reinforcement Activities — 8th Grade Math

JUMP INTO FUNCTIONS

A character named Jack made candlestick-jumping famous. Jump right into these functions problems.

Answer each question *yes* or *no*.

1. Jack jumps over candlesticks at a rate of one per second. Is the number of sticks jumped a function of the time?

2. When Sam attends the candlestick-jumping competition, he parks in the arena parking lot. It costs $3 to park 1 hour, $6 to park 2 hours, $9 to park 3 hours, and $12 to park 4 or more hours. Does this situation represent a function? Explain your answer.

3. The sports shop is having a sale on candlesticks. They cost $6 a dozen. Is the cost of candles a function of the number of dozens someone buys?

4. **y** has a constant value of 16, but **x** can be either zero or one. Is **y** a function of **x**?

5. In the equation $x = y^2 - 1$, is **y** a function of **x**?

6. In the equation $y = \frac{1}{2} x - \frac{1}{3}$, is **y** a function of **x**?

7. Is **y** a function of **x** in the equation $y = x^3$?

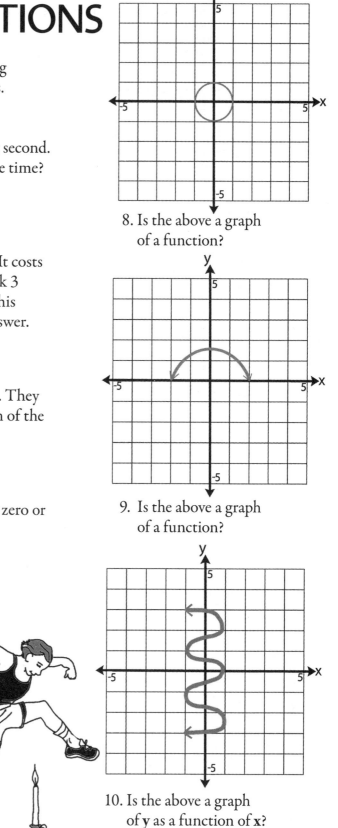

8. Is the above a graph of a function?

9. Is the above a graph of a function?

10. Is the above a graph of **y** as a function of **x**?

Name

SIDE-BY-SIDE FUNCTIONS

Delve deeper into functions! Compare different functions represented in different ways.

Answer the question or follow the instructions in each problem.

1. Two planes carrying dancers from the dance competition start from the same airport at the same time and fly in opposite directions. Assume that each flies at a constant speed. The speed of the faster plane is 100 miles per hour faster than that of the slower plane. At the end of 5 hours, they are 2,000 miles apart. What is the speed of each plane?

2. Function **f** is given by the graph at the right. Function **g** is given by the equation: $g(x) = -\frac{3}{2}x + 1$.

Circle statements that are true:

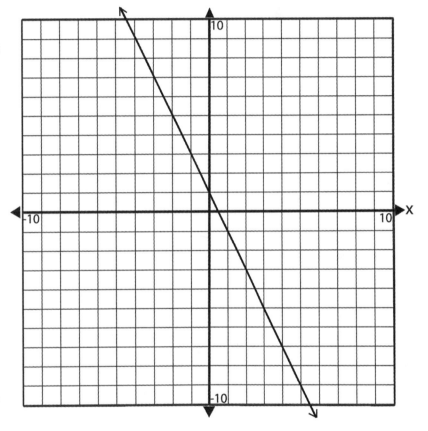

a. **f** and **g** are both increasing, and **f** is increasing faster than **g**.

b. **f** and **g** are both increasing, and **g** is increasing faster than **f**.

c. **f** and **g** are both decreasing, and **f** is decreasing faster than **g**.

d. **f** and **g** are both decreasing, and **g** is decreasing faster than **f**.

e. **f** is increasing, but **g** is decreasing.

3. For **f** and **g**, **f** is a linear function given by the table, and **g** is a function given by the equation $g(x) = 0.5x - 1$.

Which function has the smallest y-intercept?

x	y
-2	-4
-1	-3
0	-2
1	-1

Name

Use with page 66 and 67.

Common Core Reinforcement Activities — 8th Grade Math

Delve deeper into functions! Compare different functions represented in different ways.

Answer the question or follow the instructions in each problem.

4. On their way to the all-star dance team competition, the Hip Hoppers Dance Team traveled 1,200 miles in two stages—one by train and the other by plane. The train's speed was 30 miles per hour; the plane traveled at 150 miles per hour. The train portion of the trip took 2 hours longer than the plane portion. How long did the trip take (not counting any transition time or waiting time)?

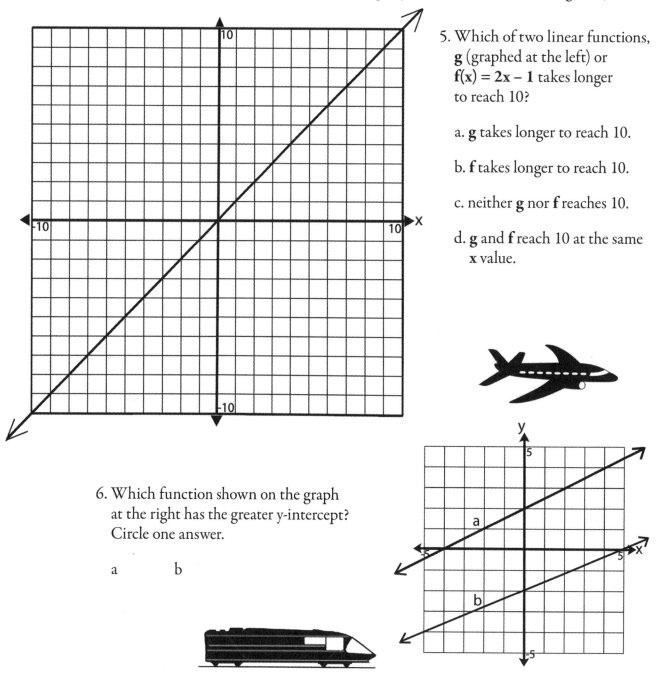

5. Which of two linear functions, **g** (graphed at the left) or **f(x) = 2x – 1** takes longer to reach 10?

   a. **g** takes longer to reach 10.

   b. **f** takes longer to reach 10.

   c. neither **g** nor **f** reaches 10.

   d. **g** and **f** reach 10 at the same **x** value.

6. Which function shown on the graph at the right has the greater y-intercept? Circle one answer.

   a   b

Delve deeper into more functions! Compare different functions represented in different ways.
Answer the question or follow the instructions in each problem.

7. **f** is a linear function given by
$$f(x) = 3(1 - x) + 4.$$

A table of values for other linear functions is given to the right. Which of these functions are decreasing faster than **f**? Circle all that apply.

x	a	b	c	d
0	0	0	0	10
1	-1	-2	-4	-5
2	-2	-4	-8	-20

a   b   c   d

8. **f** is a linear function whose table of values is shown below. Which of the functions graphed below are increasing faster than **f**? Circle all that apply:

a   b   c   d

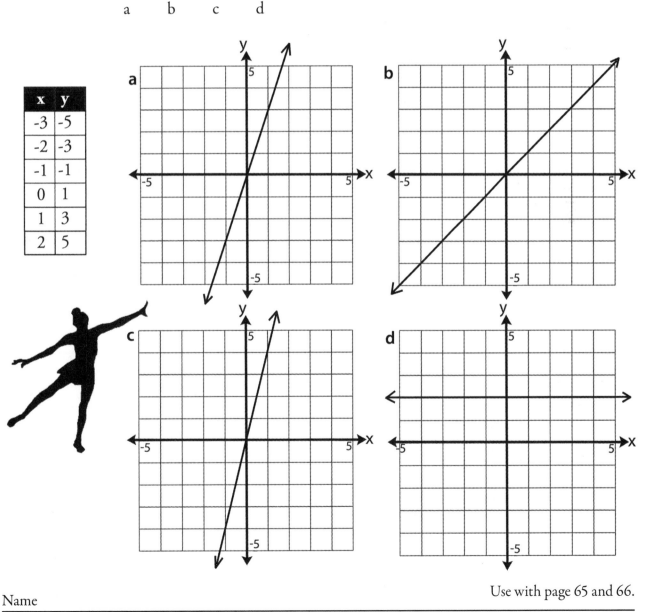

x	y
-3	-5
-2	-3
-1	-1
0	1
1	3
2	5

Use with page 65 and 66.

Name

Copyright © 2014 World Book, Inc./
Incentive Publications, Chicago, IL

Common Core Reinforcement Activities — 8th Grade Math

DIVE!

Dive right into these problems. Consider whether the equations, tables, and graphs represent linear or nonlinear relationships.

Answer each question *yes* or *no*. Give equations and explanations where instructed.

1. Skydiver Zoey (**y**) is 9 less than 3 times the age of fellow skydiver Travis (**x**). Write an equation for this sentence. Does the sentence describe a linear function?

2. The area of a triangle is $A = \frac{1}{2}bh$. For a given area, are **b** and **h** in a linear relationship?

3. Does the table represent a linear relationship?

x	y
2	5
5	10
8	15
11	16

4. Is graph A the graph of a linear function?

   Explain your answer.

5. Skydiver Lulu (**y**) takes 4 more than twice as many jumps a year as her friend Cassie (**x**). Write an equation for this sentence. Does the sentence describe a linear function?

6. Does the table represent a linear relationship?

   Explain your answer.

x	y
0	1
-1	0
1	2
2	3
-2	-1

7. Is graph B the graph of a linear function? Explain your answer.

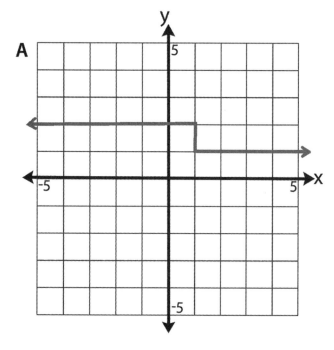

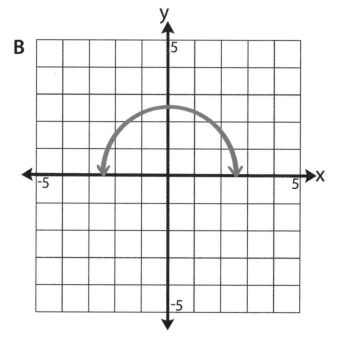

Name

Use with page 69.

SPLATS AND SLOPES

Watch out for splattering paintballs as you consider slopes and other relationships in these functions!

Follow the directions and answer the questions.

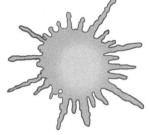

1. Entrance to a paintball court costs $6. A ticket plus 5 balls costs $8. Circle all the statements that apply to this relationship.

    a. The relationship is proportional.

    b. When the number of balls increases by 20, the price increases by $8.

    c. When the x-axis represents the number of balls, the slope of the graph of the relationship is $\frac{5}{2}$.

    d. Entrance with 10 balls costs $11.

2. What is the slope of a line that passes through the points (4, 3) and (-2, -1)?

3. Which graph represents an undefined slope?

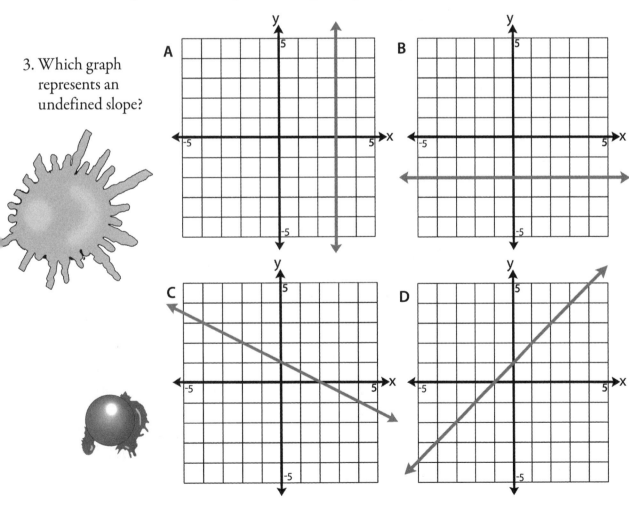

THREE TIMES THE SKILL

To complete a triathlon, an athlete performs in three rigorous competitions, usually without a break between events. This takes triple the skill and triple the practice.

Use your skills to model linear relationships three ways: with equations, graphs, and tables.

1. At the start of a long training session to prepare for a triathlon, Elijah weighed 120 pounds. At the end of 3 **hours**, he weighed 115 pounds. Assuming he was losing weight at a constant rate, which equation could represent his weight (w) as a function of time in **minutes** passed (t)? (Circle one answer.)

a. $w = 115 - 3t$
b. $w = 120 - \frac{1}{36}t$
c. $w = 120 + \frac{1}{3}t$
d. $w = 120 - \frac{3}{5}t$

2. Which function corresponds to the graph?
a. $y = \frac{1}{2}x - 1$
b. $y = \frac{1}{3}x - 1$
c. $y = \frac{1}{2}x$
d. $y = \frac{1}{2}x + 1$

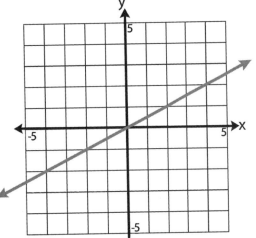

3. What is the x-intercept of $3y + 2x = 6$?

4. Given the line $y = mx + b$, what is the y-intercept?

5. What is the slope of the line represented by the following table?

x	y
0	3
1	5

6. Graph $y = 2x - 2$

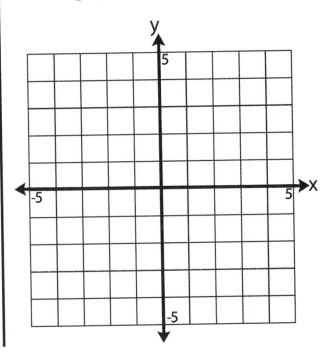

Name

THE GRAPH SPEAKS

Graphs can speak volumes. Let the graphs show the functions and give clues to the equations.

Follow the directions in each problem.

1. Jenna works as a trainer for competitive rope jumpers. She is paid $40 a session. In addition, she gets approximately $5 in tips for every client she trains during the session. Let **x** represent the number of clients Jenna trains during a session and **y** represent her income for the session. Use graph A to graph Jenna's session income as a function of the number of her clients.

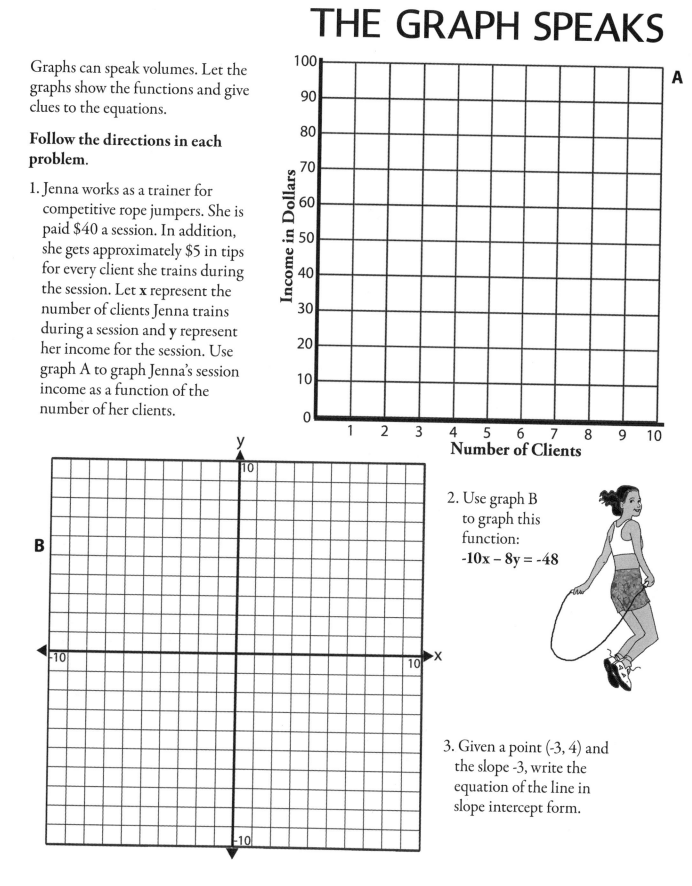

A

Income in Dollars

Number of Clients

y

B

x

2. Use graph B to graph this function:
-10x − 8y = -48

3. Given a point (-3, 4) and the slope -3, write the equation of the line in slope intercept form.

Name

Common Core Reinforcement Activities — 8th Grade Math

TRAVELING PROBLEMS

Travel problems often involve linear relationships. In two of these problems, cyclists travel in straight lines toward each other or away from each other.

Follow the directions to find or show linear relationships.

1. Two motorcyclists start from the same place at the same time. They travel in opposite directions, at speeds of 40 miles per hour and 20 miles per hour, until they are 420 miles apart. Find the time that each one travels.

2. Two bikers are biking toward each other until they meet. Biker A travels at a rate of 5 kilometers per hour and biker B travels at 6 kilometers per hour. If they were 44 kilometers apart at the start, when will they meet and how far will each one have traveled when they meet?

3. Find the equation of the line with slope -2 that passes through point (-1, 3).

4. Find the equation of the line that passes through points (2, 6) and (-2, 8).

5. Graph the following function:

   $y = f(x) = -3x - 6$

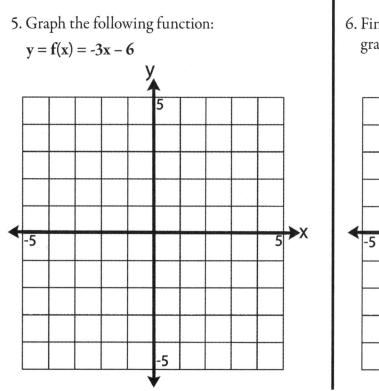

6. Find the slope of the line in the graph below.

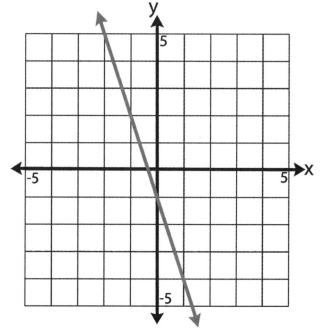

Name

GETTING OUT OF DODGE

Gunsmoke was one of the longest-running series in television history. Legendary Matt Dillon, a United States marshal and the lead character, kept law and order in the town of Dodge City, Kansas. A theme of the ongoing story was that troublemakers should get out of Dodge, if they did not want to end up in a gunfight with Matt Dillon. (Dillon always won.) The phrase "Get out of Dodge" has come to mean "leave a situation right away."

Solve the "getting out of Dodge" problem.

1. Matt is trying to get out of Dodge on his horse that is stabled on the outer border of Dodge. The table represents this situation. Let **D** = distance from the center of Dodge and **t** = time on his horse. Assume the horse travels at a constant speed. Circle all that apply:

   a. Matt's horse is called Rodney.

   b. The stable is one mile from the center of Dodge.

   c. Matt's horse travels toward Dodge at 3 mph.

   d. Matt's horse travels away from Dodge at 3 mph.

D	t
1	0
7	2
13	4

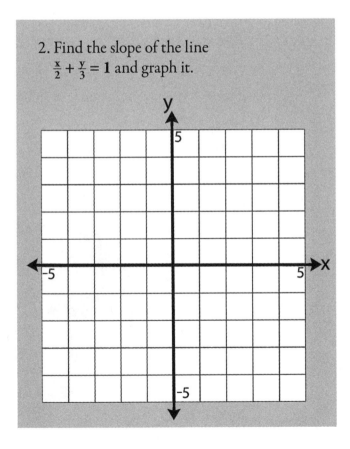

2. Find the slope of the line $\frac{x}{2} + \frac{y}{3} = 1$ and graph it.

3. Find the equation of the line that passes through (1, -16) and has slope **m**.

4. Find the slope, x-intercept, and y-intercept of $y = \frac{5}{2}x$.

   slope =

   x-intercept =

   y-intercept =

Name

THE CHANGING SLOPE

Pay close attention to the slope here! It will give you clues about function and the relationships between the values.

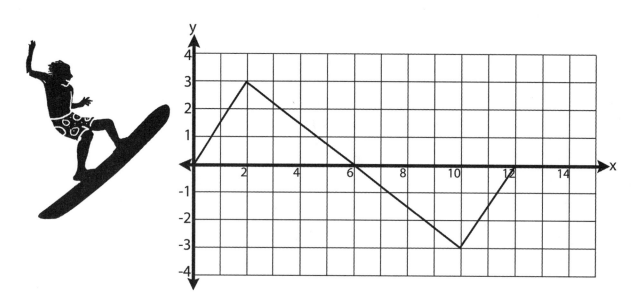

For problems 1-4, circle the correct answer.

1. Initially, as **x** increases, **y**

   a. increases

   b. decreases

2. From **x = 2** to **x = 10**, **y**

   a. increases

   b. decreases

3. For x between **x = 0** and **x = 6**,

   a. y ≤ 0   c. y ≥ 0

   b. y < 0   d. y > 0

4. For x between **x = 6** and **x = 12**,

   a. y ≤ 0   c. y ≥ 0

   b. y < 0   d. y > 0

For problems 5-6, write the correct answer in the blank.

5. Between **x = 0** and **x = 2**, the slope of the graph is equal to _____.

6. Between **x = 2** and **x = 10**, the slope of the graph is equal to _____.

Name _____

GEOMETRY

Grade 8

There has to be a way
to make this work.

A Square
Peg
in a
Round Hole

EN GARDE!

Fencing was an event at the first Modern Olympic Games in 1896. It is an old sport that was first recorded in Europe around 1400. Fencers use different kinds of swords: the foil, the épée, and the sabre. The sport takes skill and practice. A **bout** is a fight between two competing fencers. When the bout director calls "en garde," the competitors take a ready position. They begin the bout when the director gives the command: "fence."

Practice your geometry skills with these questions about congruence, similarity, and transformations of geometric figures. Continue with the questions on page 77.

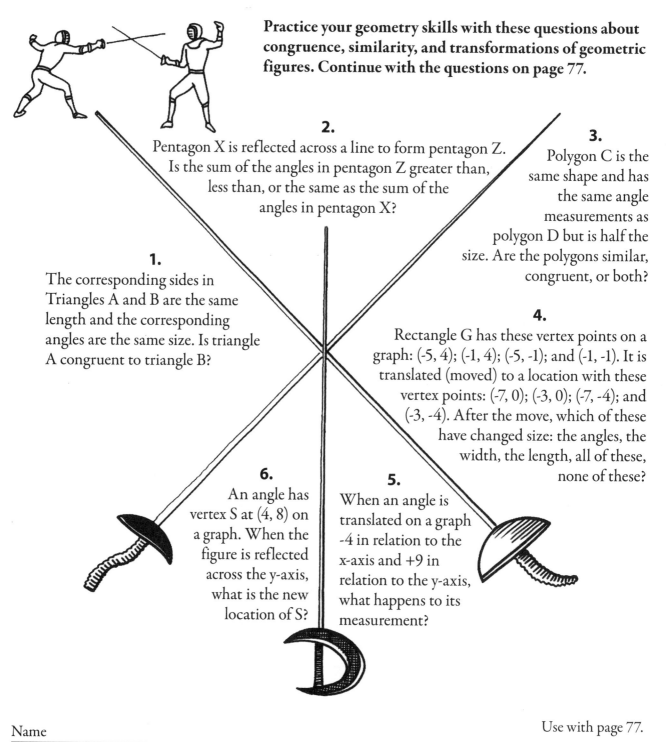

2.
Pentagon X is reflected across a line to form pentagon Z. Is the sum of the angles in pentagon Z greater than, less than, or the same as the sum of the angles in pentagon X?

3.
Polygon C is the same shape and has the same angle measurements as polygon D but is half the size. Are the polygons similar, congruent, or both?

1.
The corresponding sides in Triangles A and B are the same length and the corresponding angles are the same size. Is triangle A congruent to triangle B?

4.
Rectangle G has these vertex points on a graph: (-5, 4); (-1, 4); (-5, -1); and (-1, -1). It is translated (moved) to a location with these vertex points: (-7, 0); (-3, 0); (-7, -4); and (-3, -4). After the move, which of these have changed size: the angles, the width, the length, all of these, none of these?

6.
An angle has vertex S at (4, 8) on a graph. When the figure is reflected across the y-axis, what is the new location of S?

5.
When an angle is translated on a graph -4 in relation to the x-axis and +9 in relation to the y-axis, what happens to its measurement?

Use with page 77.

Practice your geometry skills with these questions about congruence, similarity, and transformations of geometric figures, continued from page 76.

7. A right triangle has vertices at (0, 0), (5, 0), and (5, 4). When it is rotated -270°, in what quadrant(s) will it lie? Circle all that apply: I, II, III, IV.

8. Triangle K has two angles measuring 85° and 80°. What is the measure of the third angle?

9. Two parallel lines are rotated 90° around the origin on a graph. What happens to the lines as a result? Circle all that apply: they intersect; they get closer together; they get farther apart; all of these; none of these.

10. Triangle P has angles that measure 104°, 20°, and 56°. Triangle Q is similar to and $\frac{2}{3}$ the size of triangle P. What are the measures of its angles?

11. A line segment with endpoints A (-3, -8) and B (4, -6) is reflected across a line y = -1. Where is B after the reflection?

12. Two parallel lines are translated -6 in the x direction and +5 in the y direction. What is the resulting figure?

Name

Use with page 76.

Common Core Reinforcement Activities — 8th Grade Math

SLIDES, FLIPS, AND TURNS

Geometric figures are on the move—just like athletes! They change position with movements called **transformations**. There are three types of transformations. In a **translation**, a figure slides to a new position. In a **rotation**, the figure turns—usually around a particular point. In a **reflection**, the figure is reflected (flipped) across a line.

Follow the instructions in each section to examine or create translations with lines and line segments.

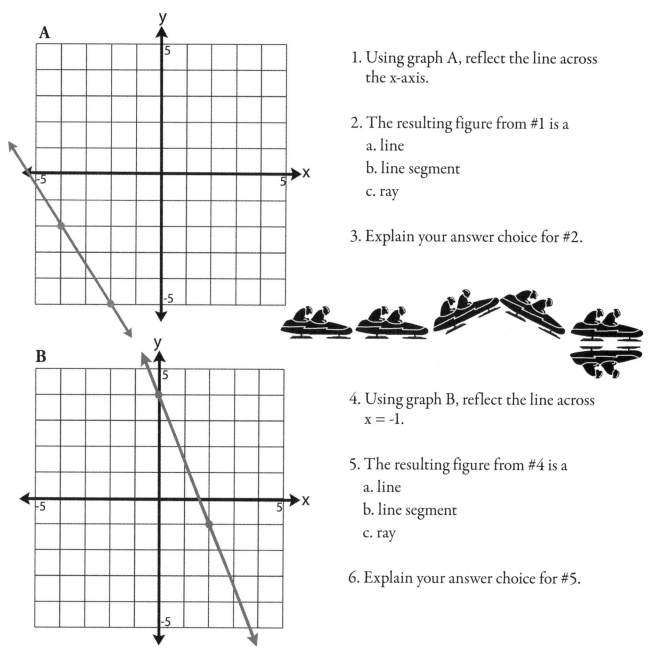

1. Using graph A, reflect the line across the x-axis.

2. The resulting figure from #1 is a
   a. line
   b. line segment
   c. ray

3. Explain your answer choice for #2.

4. Using graph B, reflect the line across x = -1.

5. The resulting figure from #4 is a
   a. line
   b. line segment
   c. ray

6. Explain your answer choice for #5.

Name

Use with page 79.

Follow the instructions in each section to examine or create translations with lines and line segments.

7. Using graph C, rotate the line -90° around the origin.

8. Label the new location for point **a** from #7 as a_1. Its coordinates are:

9. Label the new location for point **b** from #7 as b_1. Its coordinates are:

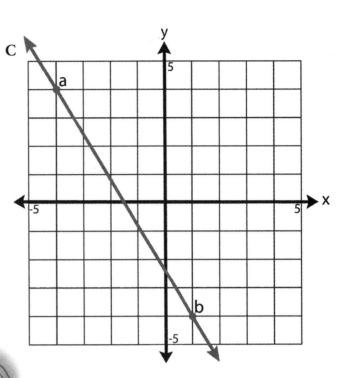

10. Using graph D, show a translation of the line, moving it +2 in relation to the x-axis and -3 in relation to the y-axis.

11. Label the new location for point **c** from #10 as c_1. Its coordinates are:

12. Label the new location for point **d** from #10 as d_1. Its coordinates are:

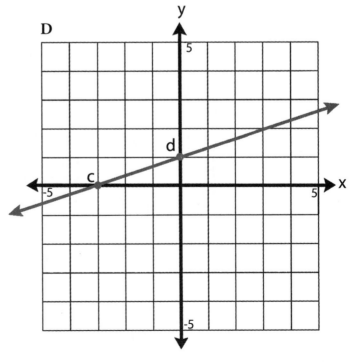

Name _____

Use with page 78.

Common Core Reinforcement Activities — 8th Grade Math

ON THE MOVE

Watch out for batons and line segments on the move!

Follow the instructions to examine or create translations with lines and line segments.

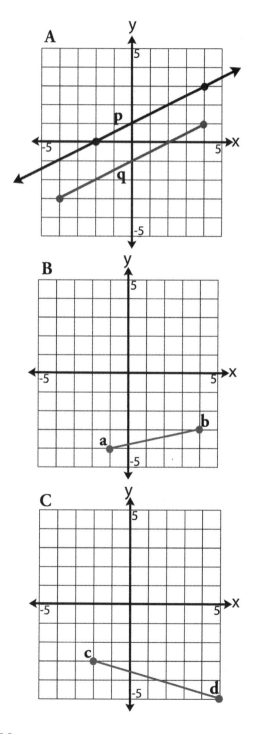

1. On graph A, is point **p** a 180° rotation of point **q** around the origin?

2. Explain why or why not (for your answer to #1).

3. Using graph B, show a translation of the line segment, moving it -3 in relation to the x-axis and +7 in relation to the y-axis.

4. Label the new location for point **a** from the translation in #3 as a_1. Its coordinates are:

5. Label the new location for point **b** from the translation in #3 as b_1. Its coordinates are:

6. Using graph C, reflect the line segment across **y = -2**. Label the new coordinates as c_1 and d_1.

7. The resulting figure from #6 is a
   a. line
   b. line segment
   c. ray

8. The resulting figure from #6 is
   a. longer than the original
   b. shorter than the original
   c. the same length as the original

Name

MENTAL GYMNASTICS

Not all gymnastics involve movement of the body. This challenge requires a nimble mind and perhaps some clever visualization. Use pencil-and-paper diagrams or graphs, if you wish.

Write T (true) or F (false) for each statement. Be ready to demonstrate or explain your answer.

_____ 1. Line segment FG has endpoints at (-8, 4) and (3, 6). When it is translated on a graph +6 in relation to the x-axis and -9 in relation to the y-axis, its new endpoints will be (2,-5) and (9, 3).

_____ 2. The vertex (B) of angle ABC is located at (-4, 5) on a graph. When the angle is rotated 270° around this vertex, its new vertex will lie at (4, -5).

_____ 3. When a line segment is translated, it becomes a line.

_____ 4. Line **g** passes through points (-5, -4) and (6, -4). After it is reflected across the x-axis, this line will not pass through quadrants III or IV on a four-quadrant graph.

_____ 5. When parallel lines are reflected across an axis, the distance between the lines decreases.

_____ 6. A line segment lies entirely in quadrant I on a graph and has endpoints **a** and **b**. When the segment is reflected across the y-axis, one or more of the endpoints will have coordinates comprised of two negative numbers.

_____ 7. The vertex (S) of angle RST has coordinates of (-6, -8). When the angle is reflected across the line y = -4, the vertex (S) will still have coordinates comprised of two negative numbers.

_____ 8. When a line is rotated around the origin, it will not necessarily have any points on the origin.

_____ 9. When an angle is both reflected and translated on a graph, the measure of its angle does not change.

_____ 10. When a line segment is reflected across the y-axis, its length increases.

_____ 11. When rotated around a point, a pair of parallel lines will eventually intersect.

_____ 12. The vertex of angle EFG is located at (0, -5) on a graph. When the angle is translated -7 in relation to the x-axis and +4 in relation to the y-axis, the entire angle will be contained within quadrant II.

Name _____

Common Core Reinforcement Activities — 8th Grade Math

AWESOME ANGLES

To master these feats and many other athletic positions, athletes move their bodies into some spectacular angles.

Show your understanding of angles on the move. Examine and draw the transformations described.

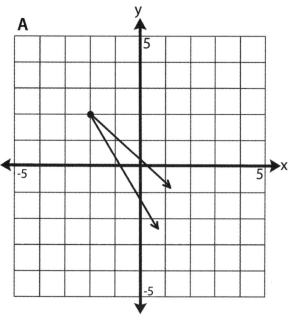

A

1. Using graph A, show a translation of the angle, moving it -3 in relation to the x-axis and -5 in relation to the y-axis.

2. On graph B, which angle is a rotation of angle Q around its vertex?
   a. angle R   c. angle S
   b. angle T   d. none of the angles

3. On graph B, is angle T a translation of angle R?
   yes   no

4. On graph B, which angle reflects angle Q across the y-axis?
   a. angle R   c. angle S
   b. angle T   d. none of the angles

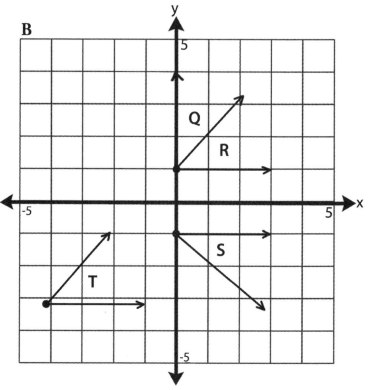

B

**Show your understanding of angles on the move.
Examine and draw the transformations described**

5. Using graph C, rotate the angle 270° around its vertex.

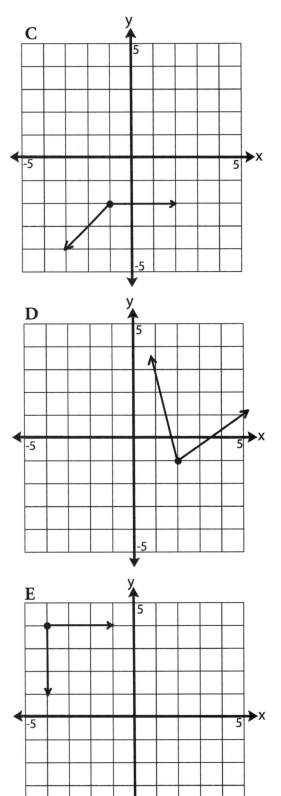

6. Using graph D, reflect the angle across the y-axis. Label this "reflection."

7. After the move in #6, what are the coordinates of the vertex?

8. Using graph D, show a translation of the original angle, moving it -2 in relation to the x-axis and -4 in relation to the y-axis.

9. Using graph E, reflect the angle across a line **x = -1**.

10. After the reflection in #9, what are the coordinates of the vertex?

11. After the reflection in #9, the measure of the angle is
   a. greater than the original
   b. less than the original
   c. the same as the original

Name _____

Use with page 82.

NO INTERSECTING SKIS!

An important skill in downhill skiing is the ability to keep the skis parallel and make turns while keeping them in a parallel position. If the skis are kept parallel, there won't be any chances of the two skis becoming intersecting lines. That can lead to trouble! When making moves with parallel lines in geometry, it is also essential to keep those lines parallel.

Follow the directions on this page and the next, page 85, to perform some translations with parallel lines.

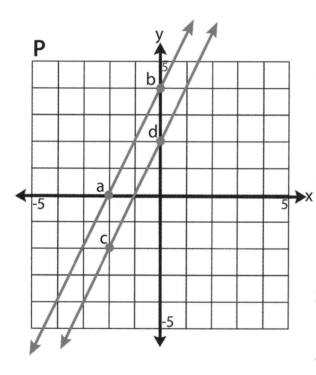

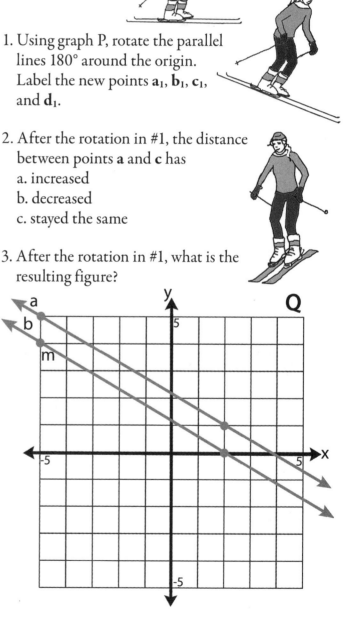

1. Using graph P, rotate the parallel lines 180° around the origin. Label the new points a_1, b_1, c_1, and d_1.

2. After the rotation in #1, the distance between points **a** and **c** has
   a. increased
   b. decreased
   c. stayed the same

3. After the rotation in #1, what is the resulting figure?

4. Using graph Q, reflect the lines across the x-axis. Label the new lines a_1 and b_1.

5. The resulting figure from #4 is
   a. two line segments
   b. two parallel lines
   c. two intersecting lines

6. After the reflection in #4, the location of point **m** is
   a. (-5, -4)
   b. (5, -4)
   c. (-5, 4)
   d. (4, -5)

Name

Use with page 84.

Uh oh!

Follow the directions on this page and the next to perform some translations with parallel lines.

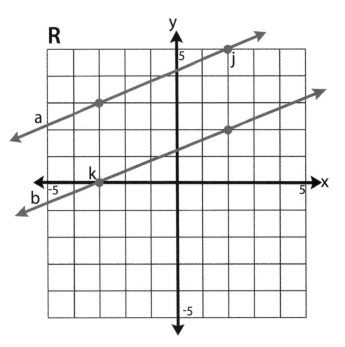

7. Using Graph R, show a translation of the lines, moving them +3 in relation to the x-axis and -4 in relation to the y-axis. Label the new lines a_1 and b_1.

8. Label the new location for point **j** from #7 as j_1. Its coordinates are:

9. Label the new location for point **k** from #7 as k_1. Its coordinates are:

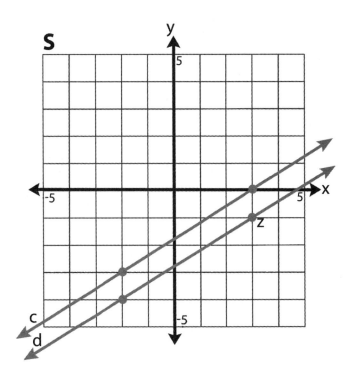

10. Using graph S, reflect the lines across the x-axis. Label the new lines c_1 and d_1.

11. The resulting figure will be
    a. one line segment
    b. two line segments
    c. two parallel lines
    d. two intersecting lines

12. After the reflection, what is the location of point **z**?

Name

Use with page 84.

Common Core Reinforcement Activities — 8th Grade Math

FIGURE THIS!

At Weaverville High School, students have been figuring out how to combine figures for a new swimming pool design. Here are some of the figures that will be part of the new look for the bottom of the pool.

Compare the figures and answer the questions.

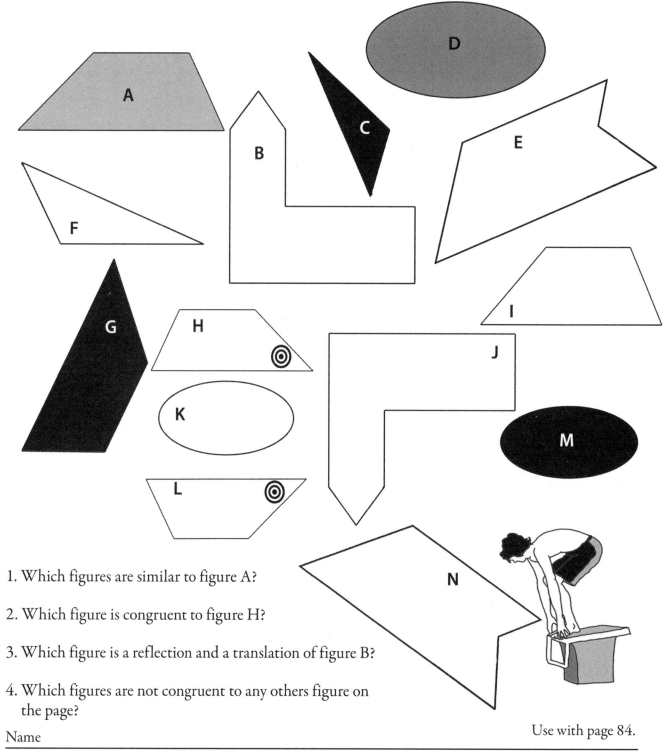

1. Which figures are similar to figure A?

2. Which figure is congruent to figure H?

3. Which figure is a reflection and a translation of figure B?

4. Which figures are not congruent to any others figure on the page?

Name _____

Use with page 84.

In each problem, the two figures are congruent. For each situation, describe the sequence of transformations by which the second figure is obtained from the first. Your description does not have to give precise measurements for transformations.

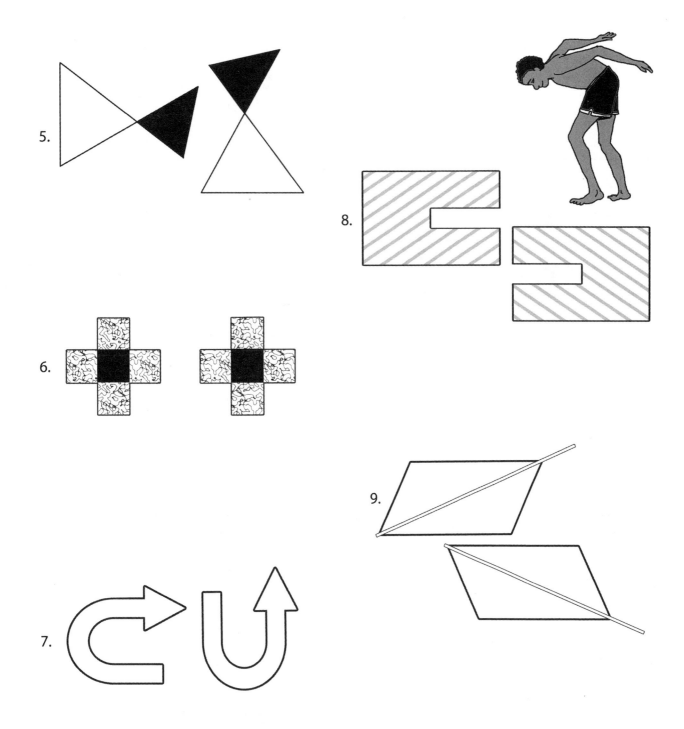

SLIDING ON THE ICE

Some things (other than skates and hockey players) are moving around on the ice at the hockey rink. A hockey stick and a team flag fell on the ice and, in the midst of all the activity, shifted around.

Follow the directions to translate the figures to new locations or positions.

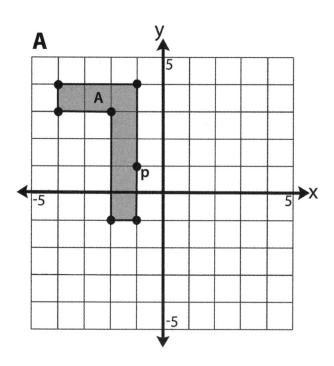

1. On graph A, rotate figure A -90° around point p at (-1, 1). Draw the figure. Label it A_1.

2. Translate figure A_1 +2 in relation to the x-axis and -6 in relation to the y-axis. Draw the figure. Label it A_2.

3. What is the location of point **p** after the rotation and the translation from #1 and #2?

4. Is the resulting figure (figure A_2 from #2) congruent to figure A?

5. On graph B, translate figure B +3 in relation to the x-axis and +5 in relation to the y-axis. Draw the figure. Label it B_1.

6. On graph B, reflect figure B_1 from #5 across the y-axis. Draw the figure. Label it B_2.

7. What is the location of point **q** after the translation and reflection from #5 and #6?

8. Is the resulting figure (figure B_2 from #6) congruent to figure B?

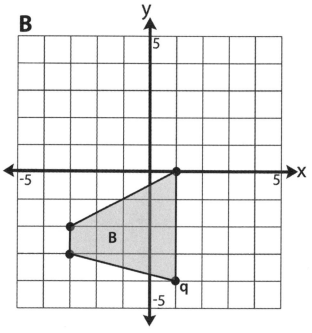

Name _____

Use with page 89.

More flags have blown onto the ice. Any one of the flags may be (or may not be) congruent to another. Use rotations, reflections, and translations to decide if figures are congruent.

Follow the directions to compare figures (flags) on the ice and answer the questions. Be ready to discuss your answers with a classmate. Explain how you can use translations, rotations, and reflections to support your answers.

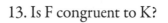

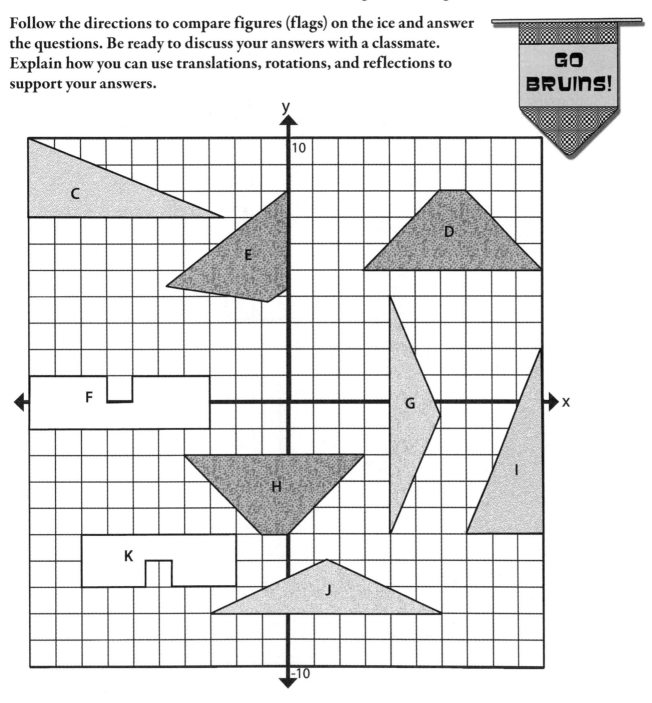

9. Is C congruent to I?

10. Is E congruent to D?

11. Is G congruent to J?

12. Is D congruent to H?

13. Is F congruent to K?

UNDERWATER MOVES

Things that fall into the sea, unless they are very heavy, are likely to be moved around by the motions of the water. Imagine the reflections, translations, and rotations of objects that might find their way to the sandy bottom of the sea.

Read the descriptions of hypothetical items in the sea. Imagine the bottom as a coordinate plane. Use the blank graphs to show how each item might lie after the described translation.

1. A flat object lies with its vertices at A (-4, -3), B (-4, -4), C (1, -4), and D (-1, -1). The water rotates the object around (-1, -1) 90°. Using graph A, draw the figure after rotation.

2. Give the coordinates of C after the rotation in #1.

3. A parallelogram-shaped figure lies with the endpoints of side PQ at (5, 3) and (5, -2). Side RS is parallel to side PQ. After a reflection of the figure over the line x = 1, the endpoints of $R_1 S_1$ lie at (0, -3) and (0, 2). Show the reflection on graph B.

4. How does the distance between sides $P_1 Q_1$ and $R_1 S_1$ compare to the distance between sides PQ and RS before the reflection from #3?

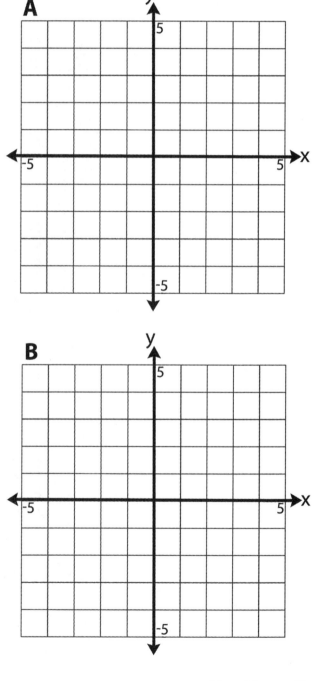

Name

Use with page 91.

Read the descriptions of hypothetical items in the sea. Imagine the bottom as a coordinate plane. Use the blank graphs to show how each item might lie after the described translation.

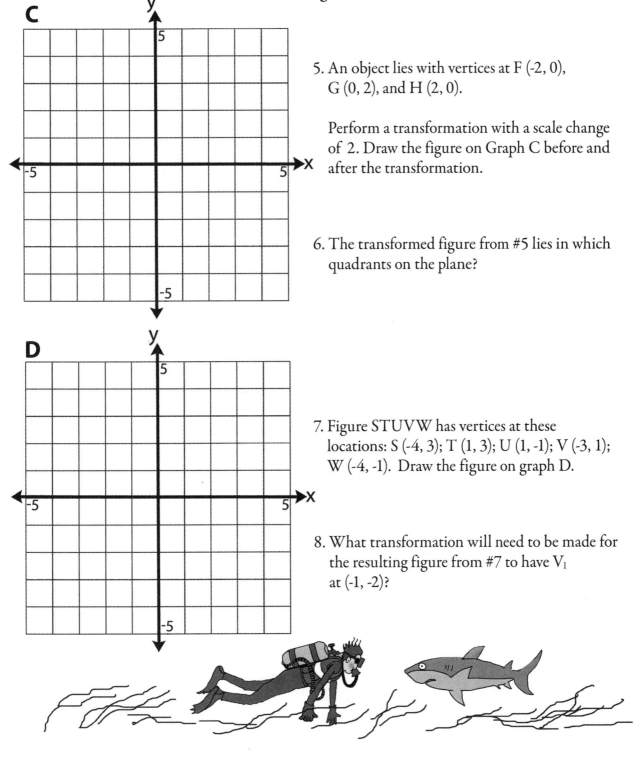

5. An object lies with vertices at F (-2, 0), G (0, 2), and H (2, 0).

   Perform a transformation with a scale change of 2. Draw the figure on Graph C before and after the transformation.

6. The transformed figure from #5 lies in which quadrants on the plane?

7. Figure STUVW has vertices at these locations: S (-4, 3); T (1, 3); U (1, -1); V (-3, 1); W (-4, -1). Draw the figure on graph D.

8. What transformation will need to be made for the resulting figure from #7 to have V_1 at (-1, -2)?

Name _____

Use with page 90.

Common Core Reinforcement Activities — 8th Grade Math

FOR THE SPORT OF IT

The pages of this catalog show some sports equipment. Look for similarity in the images. Use mental athleticism to "move" figures around to determine similarity.

Decide if the two figures in each item are similar. Explain your decisions.

1. Are figures A and B similar? Explain your answer.

Item: *soccer balls*

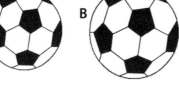

A   radius = 3.4 in
B   radius = 4.4 in

1

2. Are figures C and D similar? Explain your answer.

Item: *baseball home plates*

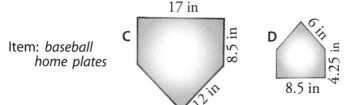

17 in
C
8.5 in
D
6 in
4.25 in
12 in
8.5 in

2

3. Are figures E and F similar? Explain your answer.

Item: *tennis rackets*

E
12 in
24 in
F
9 in
20 in

3

4. Are figures G and H similar? Explain your answer.

Item: *horse shoes*

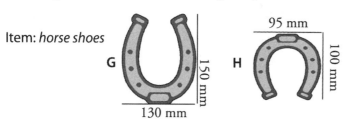

G
150 mm
130 mm
95 mm
H
100 mm

4

5. Are figures I and J similar? Explain your answer.

Item: *downhill skis*

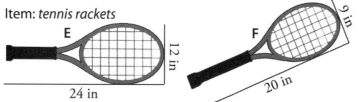

I
152 cm
72 mm
J
90 mm
190 cm

5

Name

Use with page 93.

To look for similarity in figures, move figures next to or on top of one another to compare them. You can use your pencil to draw the transformations on the graph or move the figures mentally.

Answer the question about similarity in each problem. Explain how you arrived at your answer.

6. Is figure C similar to figure D?

   Explain your decision. As a part of your explanation, describe the series of transformations you did to help make your decision.

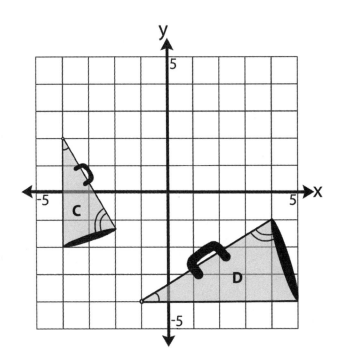

7. Is figure E similar to figure F?

   Explain your decision. As a part of your explanation, describe the series of transformations you did to help make your decision.

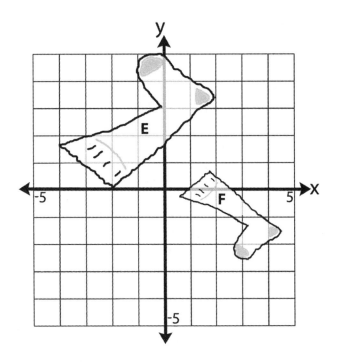

Name

Use with page 93.

Common Core Reinforcement Activities — 8th Grade Math

AN UNUSUAL ANGLE

Not all races involve humans moving at top speeds. Here's an unusual angle on racing: with some organizational help from people, spectators can enjoy watching slugs, crickets, frogs, turtles, snails, hamsters, worms, or lizards race.

Answer the questions about the angular paths of these creatures.

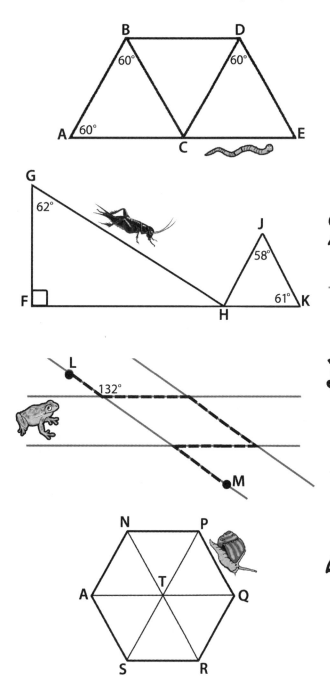

1 A worm races from C to A to B to C to E to D to B, staying on the path (lines) and making the turns at the angles. How many degrees of turns will the worm have made at the end of its route?

2 A cricket races from G to F to H to J to K to H to F, staying on the path (lines) and making the turns at the angles. How many degrees of turns will the cricket have made at the end of its route?

3 The image shows two parallel lines cutting across two parallel lines. A frog races from point L to point M, following the dotted path and making the turns at the angles. How many degrees of turns will the frog have made at the end of its route?

4 The image shows a regular hexagon. All central angles are congruent. A snail races from N to P to Q to R to T to A to S, staying on the path and making the turns at the angles. How many degrees of turns will the snail have made at the end of its route?

Name

Use with page 95.

These critters are racing along triangular paths. Some of the pairs of triangles are congruent. The chart shows the rules for proving triangle congruence.

Examine each pair of triangles. Write the letters to show which rule explains why the triangles are congruent. If none of the rules apply, write NC for *not congruent.*

ASA—angle-side-angle	A pair of corresponding angles and the included sides are equal.
SSS—side-side-side	All three corresponding sides are equal in length.
SAS—side-angle-side	A pair of corresponding sides and the included angle are equal.
AAS—angle-side-side	A pair of corresponding angles and a non-included angle are equal.
HL—hypotenuse-leg	Two right triangles are congruent if the hypotenuse and one leg are equal.

5. _____

6. _____

7. _____

8. _____

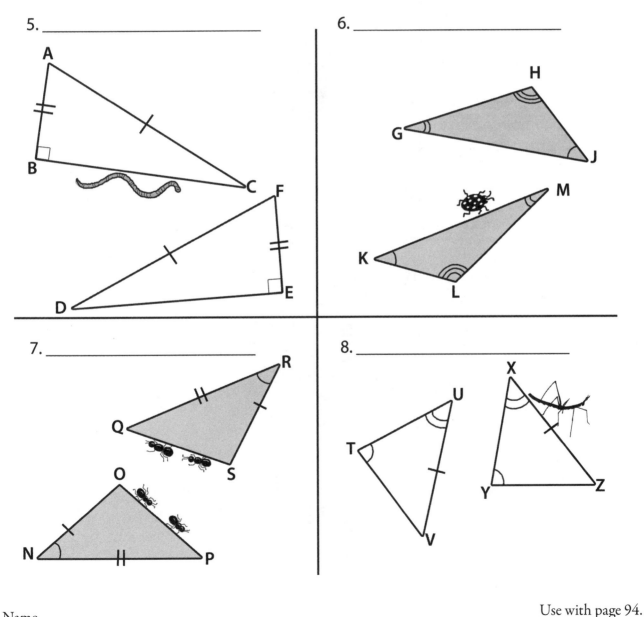

Name _____

Use with page 94.

Common Core Reinforcement Activities — 8th Grade Math

WHICH FORK?

As they practice, compete in, or enjoy their sports, many athletes follow trails. Often there will be forks in the trail and decisions to make.

For each of these situations, one fork finishes the problem correctly. Circle the right answer to choose the correct trail.

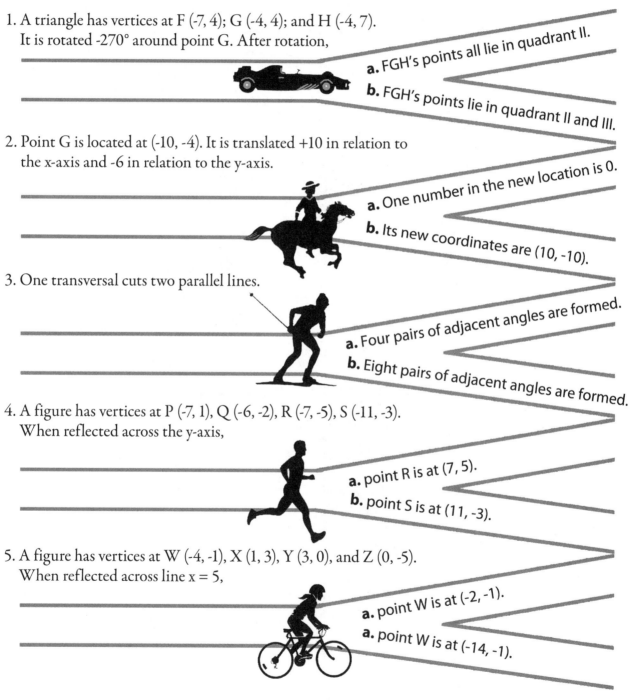

1. A triangle has vertices at F (-7, 4); G (-4, 4); and H (-4, 7). It is rotated -270° around point G. After rotation,

   a. FGH's points all lie in quadrant II.

   b. FGH's points lie in quadrant II and III.

2. Point G is located at (-10, -4). It is translated +10 in relation to the x-axis and -6 in relation to the y-axis.

   a. One number in the new location is 0.

   b. Its new coordinates are (10, -10).

3. One transversal cuts two parallel lines.

   a. Four pairs of adjacent angles are formed.

   b. Eight pairs of adjacent angles are formed.

4. A figure has vertices at P (-7, 1), Q (-6, -2), R (-7, -5), S (-11, -3). When reflected across the y-axis,

   a. point R is at (7, 5).

   b. point S is at (11, -3).

5. A figure has vertices at W (-4, -1), X (1, 3), Y (3, 0), and Z (0, -5). When reflected across line x = 5,

   a. point W is at (-2, -1).

   a. point W is at (-14, -1).

Name

Use with page 97.

**For each of these situations, one fork finishes the problem correctly.
Circle the right answer to choose the correct trail.**

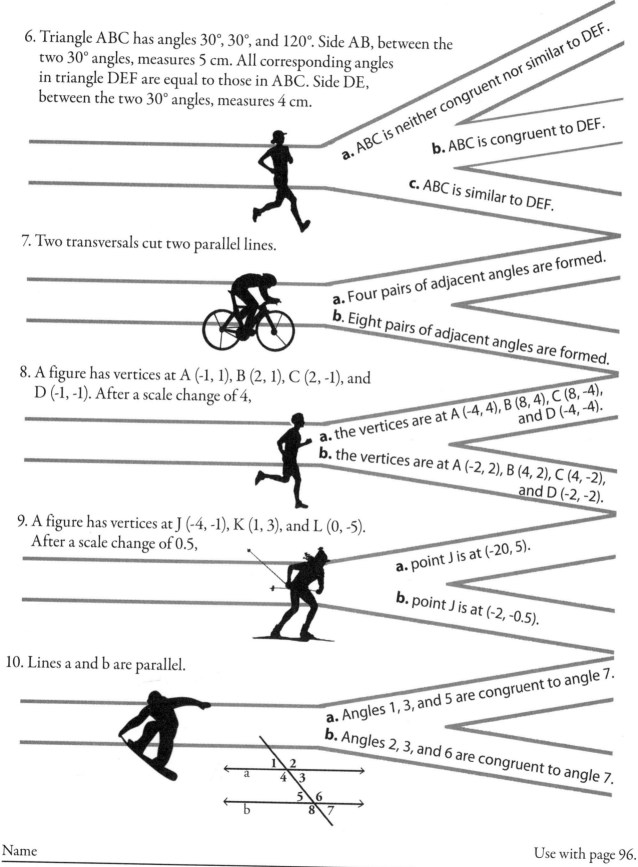

6. Triangle ABC has angles 30°, 30°, and 120°. Side AB, between the two 30° angles, measures 5 cm. All corresponding angles in triangle DEF are equal to those in ABC. Side DE, between the two 30° angles, measures 4 cm.

a. ABC is neither congruent nor similar to DEF.

b. ABC is congruent to DEF.

c. ABC is similar to DEF.

7. Two transversals cut two parallel lines.

a. Four pairs of adjacent angles are formed.

b. Eight pairs of adjacent angles are formed.

8. A figure has vertices at A (-1, 1), B (2, 1), C (2, -1), and D (-1, -1). After a scale change of 4,

a. the vertices are at A (-4, 4), B (8, 4), C (8, -4), and D (-4, -4).

b. the vertices are at A (-2, 2), B (4, 2), C (4, -2), and D (-2, -2).

9. A figure has vertices at J (-4, -1), K (1, 3), and L (0, -5). After a scale change of 0.5,

a. point J is at (-20, 5).

b. point J is at (-2, -0.5).

10. Lines a and b are parallel.

a. Angles 1, 3, and 5 are congruent to angle 7.

b. Angles 2, 3, and 6 are congruent to angle 7.

Name

Use with page 96.

Common Core Reinforcement Activities — 8th Grade Math

PROVING PYTHAGORAS'S IDEA

About 250 years after the ancient Greeks began the tradition of Olympic Games, a Greek mathematician became fascinated with right triangles. Pythagoras was not the only one to notice a special relationship between the sides of a right triangle, but the theorem that states the relationship was given his name.

Help to explain the proving of the Pythagorean Theorem by answering each of the four WHY questions as you work through its proof.

GIVEN: a right triangle with sides a and b and hypotenuse c

PROVE: $a^2 + b^2 = c^2$

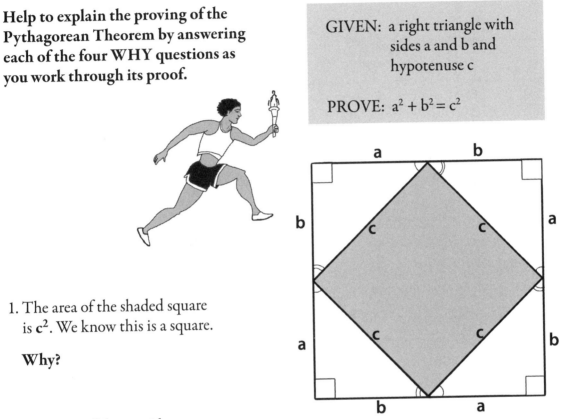

1. The area of the shaded square is c^2. We know this is a square.

   Why?

2. The area of the outside square is $(a + b)^2$. Each of the four triangles is congruent to the other.

   Why?

3. The area of the shaded square equals the area of the outside square minus the area of the four triangles. The area of the four triangles is $4 \cdot \frac{1}{2} ab$.

   Why?

4. Therefore, the area of the shaded square is $(a + b)^2 - (4 \cdot \frac{1}{2} ab) = c^2$ and this is equal to

   $a^2 + 2ab + b^2 - 2ab = c^2$.

   Why?

   Therefore, the equation above simplifies to

   $a^2 + b^2 = c^2$

   which is what we set out to prove. So we're done!

Name

PROVING THE CONVERSE

The Pythagorean Theorem proves the unique relationship between the three sides of a right triangle. Quite conveniently, the converse, or reverse, of the theorem can be proved as well. If a triangle has sides a, b, and c where $a^2 + b^2 = c^2$, then the triangle is a right triangle.

GIVEN: triangle ABC with sides a, b, and c, and $a^2 + b^2 = c^2$

PROVE: triangle ABC is a right triangle

Help to explain how the converse of the Pythagorean Theorem is proved. Give the reason for each step in the proof.

Consider another triangle **XYZ** which is a right triangle with sides **a** and **b** equal to **a** and **b** in triangle **ABC**.

Side **z** is the hypotenuse of triangle **XYZ**.

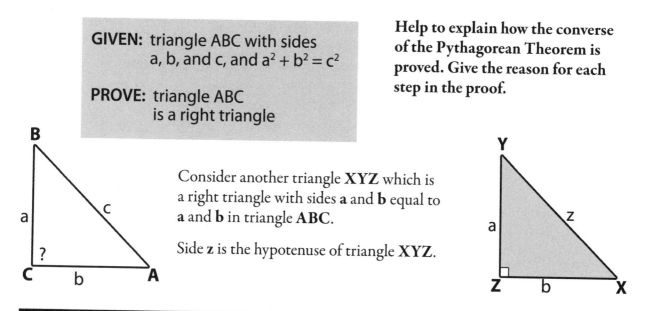

	Step in Proof	Reason
1	$a^2 + b^2 = z^2$	
2	$a^2 + b^2 = c^2$	
3	$z^2 = c^2$	
4	$z = c$	
5	Δ ABC is congruent to Δ XYZ	
6	∠ c is congruent to right ∠ z	
7	∠ c is a right angle and ΔABC is a right Δ	

Name

Common Core Reinforcement Activities — 8th Grade Math

RAMP IT UP

A much sought-after record is the longest motorcycle ramp jump. Robbie Maddison, of Australia, set a Guinness World Record in 2008 with a jump of 106.98 meters (351 ft). Unlike traditional motorcycle-jumping ramps, these don't have a curve at the top. Instead, they are perfect right triangles.

One measurement is missing from each ramp. The missing measurements are shown in the puffs of bike exhaust below. All measurements are meters. Write the letter of the ramp next to the missing measurement. (The triangles are not necessarily proportional.)

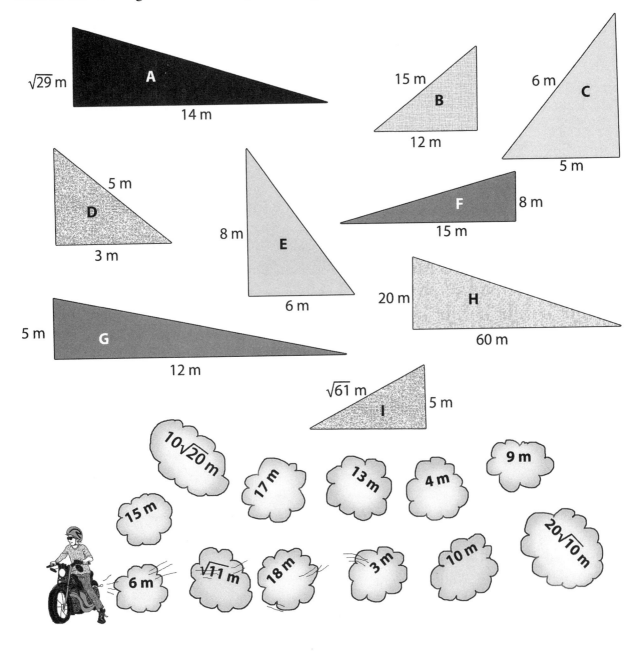

Name

OUT OF THE SHADOWS

As dusk falls, Detective Zeke gets a call about a robbery at a neighborhood sports center. When he gets to the scene, a neighbor said she saw a shadowy figure carrying a huge bag hiding near a lamppost against a building nearby. The witness told Detective Zeke that she noticed how the shadow of the figure reached just to the edge of the sidewalk.

Solve the problems about these mysterious circumstances.

1. Investigators measured to find the distances. Four suspects were apprehended—all of whom had a large number of basketballs in their vehicles. The heights of the suspects were:

   Lou: 6 ft, 9 in   Axel: 4 ft, 10 in

   Maxi: 5 ft, 7 in   Sue: 6 ft

   Which suspect could have been the shadowy figure?

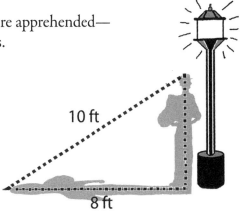

10 ft

8 ft

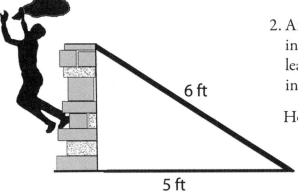

6 ft

5 ft

2. Another witness reported seeing a person, dressed in dark clothing and carrying a large, bulky bag, leap up on a wall and slide down an embankment in the park.

   How tall was the wall?

3. Detective Zeke consults many books to help him with investigations. This stack of books includes geometry tricks to help with measurements and calculations.

   How tall is the stack of books?

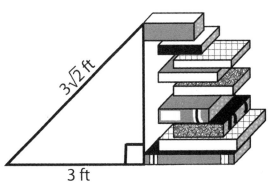

$3\sqrt{2}$ ft

3 ft

Name

Common Core Reinforcement Activities — 8th Grade Math

UNEXPECTED IMPEDIMENTS

Two friends, Destiny and Abigail, encountered unexpected impediments in the course of their athletic pursuits. The Pythagorean Theorem will help you solve the problems about these unwanted "adventures."

Solve the distance problems on this page and the next, page 103.

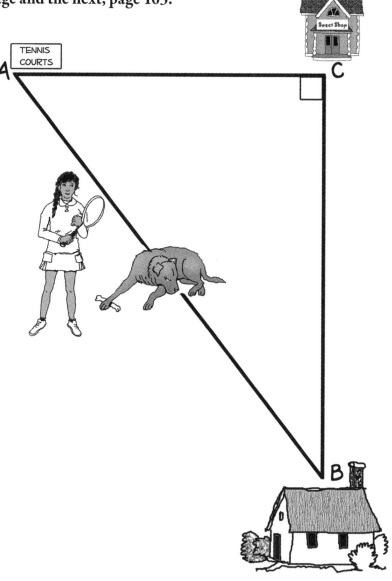

1. On her way home from tennis practice, Destiny had walked exactly halfway along the path from A to B when she heard a snore. Meatball, the dog that ferociously guarded the nearby chocolate shop, blocked her way. She had tangled with Meatball before and was too tired to run from him today. She hurried back to the tennis court and took another route home, walking 30 meters from A to C (the chocolate shop). From there, she walked 40 meters to her home at point B. She was just about to settle in for a snack when she realized she had left her cell phone at the court. To avoid running into Meatball again, she took the long way from B to C to A both ways—back to the courts and home again. How far did Destiny walk?

Name

Use with page 103.

Solve the distance problems on this page and the previous page, page 102.

2. Scuba diver Josephine is moving along the sea floor when she spots a sunken chest. She wants to explore this chest, which is this distance away: $100\sqrt{2}$. But an elephant seal bars her from proceeding to the chest. She swims along the sea floor x meters in the direction from A to B and another distance x in the direction B to C, making a right-angle turn at B. How far does Josephine swim, while keeping an eye on the seal?

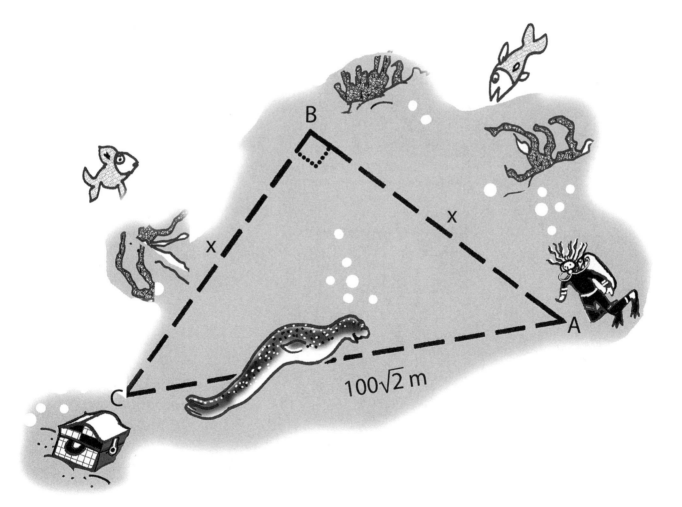

$100\sqrt{2}$ m

Name

Use with page 102.

LONG-DISTANCE SLIDING

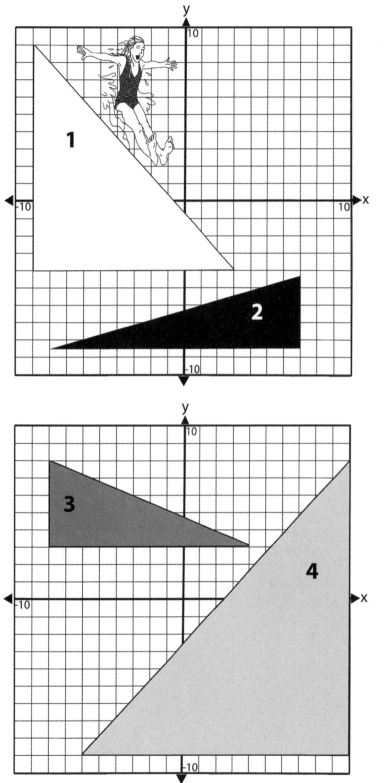

The Summit Plummet in Blizzard Beach, a Florida water park, is a 120-foot-high (36.6-meter-high) waterslide. The park claims that it is one of the tallest and fastest free-fall body slides in the world.

Find the length of the slides on each grid. Triangles are not to scale.

1. What is the length of the slide (hypotenuse) in figure 1?

2. What is the length of the slide (hypotenuse) in figure 2?

3. What is the length of the slide (hypotenuse) in figure 3?

4. If the scale of this graph is 1 unit = 3 meters, what is the height of this waterslide (figure 4)?

   What is its length (hypotenuse to scale)?

Name

Use with page 105.

Pythagorean Theorem, Problem Solving

Find the length of the slides on each grid. Triangles are not to scale.

5. What is the length of the slide (hypotenuse) in figure 5?

6. If the scale of slide 6 is 1 unit = 10 feet, is this slide higher than Florida's Summit Plummit? (See page 104.)

   What is its length (hypotenuse to scale)?

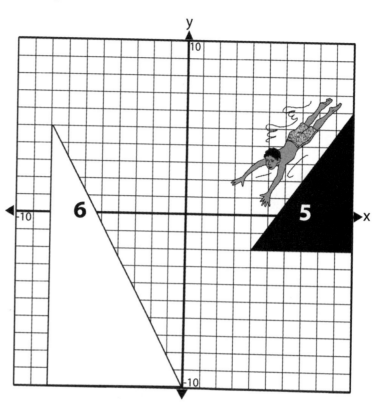

7. What is the length of the slide (hypotenuse) in figure 7?

8. What is the length of the slide (hypotenuse) in figure 8?

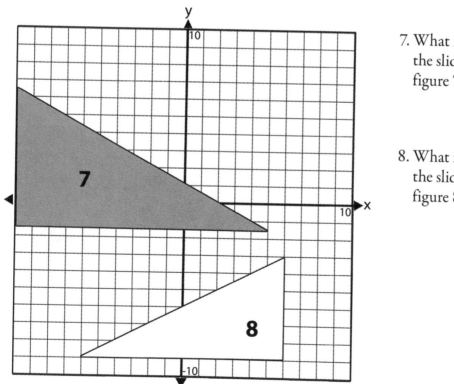

Name

Use with page 104.

Common Core Reinforcement Activities — 8th Grade Math

SPORTS AND SNACKS

Sports and snacks go together! Find the volume of some sports items and the volume of some of the snacks and drinks enjoyed before, during, and after the sporting events.

Find the missing measurement in each problem. Use 3.14 for pi.

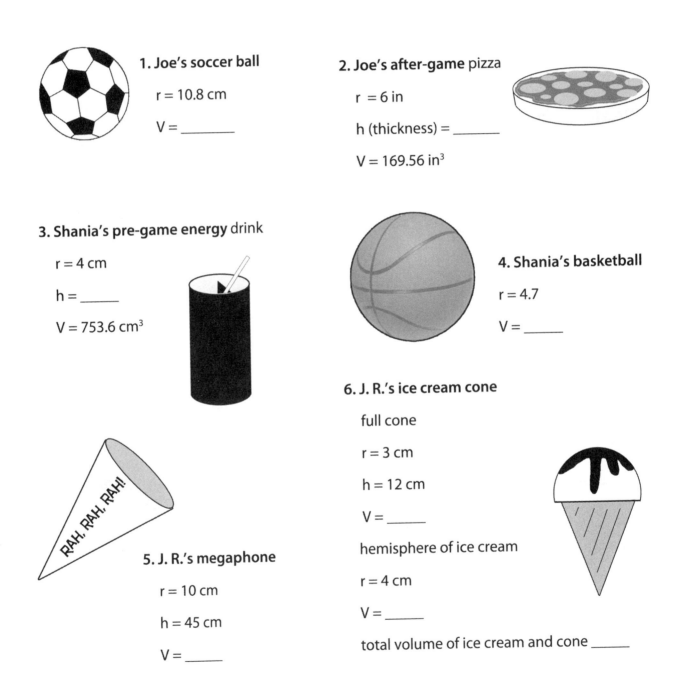

1. Joe's soccer ball

r = 10.8 cm

V = _____

2. Joe's after-game pizza

r = 6 in

h (thickness) = _____

V = 169.56 in³

3. Shania's pre-game energy drink

r = 4 cm

h = _____

V = 753.6 cm³

4. Shania's basketball

r = 4.7

V = _____

6. J. R.'s ice cream cone

full cone

r = 3 cm

h = 12 cm

V = _____

hemisphere of ice cream

r = 4 cm

V = _____

total volume of ice cream and cone _____

5. J. R.'s megaphone

r = 10 cm

h = 45 cm

V = _____

RAH, RAH, RAH!

Use with page 107.

Name

Volume: Cylinders, Cones, and Spheres

Find the missing measurement in each problem. Use 3.14 for pi.

7. **Yolanda's yoyo**

r = 4.5 cm

h = 5 cm

V = _____

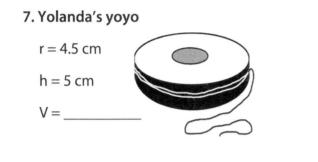

8. **Yolanda's warm-up hot chocolate**

r = 3.8 cm

h = 10

V = _____

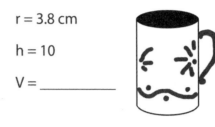

9. **cone for track team obstacle course**

r = 10 in

h = 35 in

V = _____

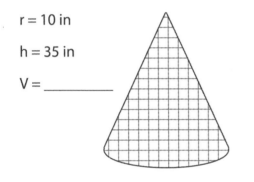

10. **the track team's water jug**

r = _____

h = 60 cm

V = 75,360 cm³

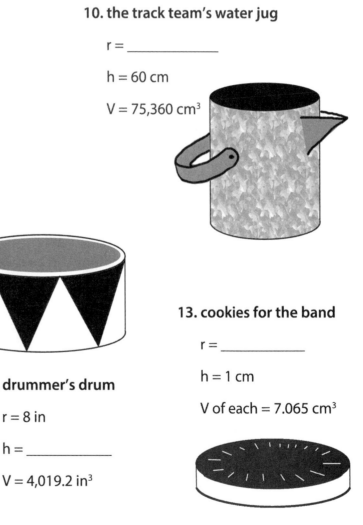

11. **drummer's drumsticks**

r = 0.6 cm

h = 25 cm

V of each = _____

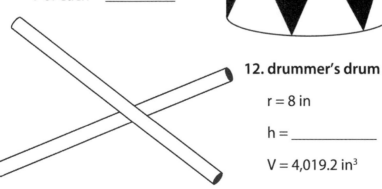

12. **drummer's drum**

r = 8 in

h = _____

V = 4,019.2 in³

13. **cookies for the band**

r = _____

h = 1 cm

V of each = 7.065 cm³

Use with page 106.

Name

Common Core Reinforcement Activities — 8th Grade Math

THE SPHERES OF SPORTS

Many sports involve actions with spheres that bounce, roll, soar, or ricochet. Focus on the different sizes and volumes of these essential sports items.

All the balls pictured are spheres. Find the volume for each sphere in terms of π. (d = diameter and r = radius.) The sizes shown here are not proportional to actual sizes. Round answers to the nearest hundredth.

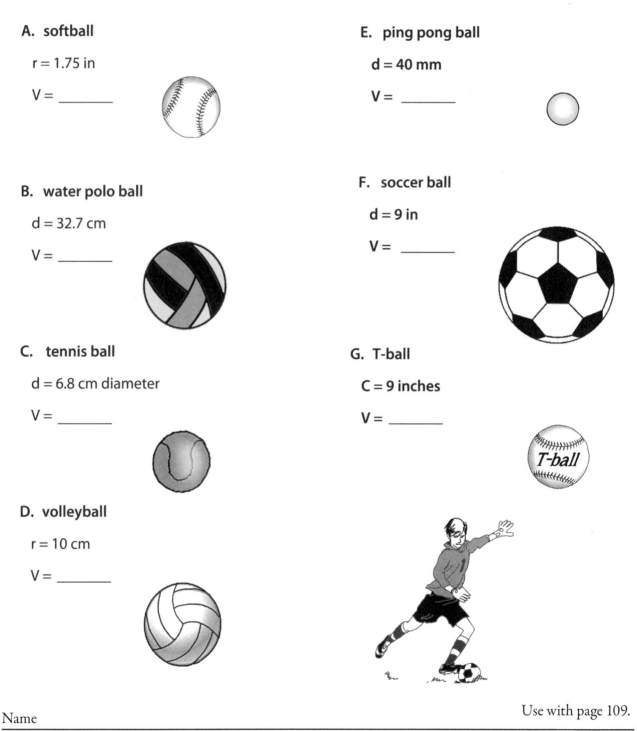

A. softball

r = 1.75 in

V = _____

B. water polo ball

d = 32.7 cm

V = _____

C. tennis ball

d = 6.8 cm diameter

V = _____

D. volleyball

r = 10 cm

V = _____

E. ping pong ball

d = 40 mm

V = _____

F. soccer ball

d = 9 in

V = _____

G. T-ball

C = 9 inches

V = _____

Name _____

Use with page 109.

**All the balls pictured are spheres. Find the volume for each sphere in terms of π.
(d = diameter and r = radius.) The sizes shown here are not proportional to actual sizes.
Round answers to the nearest hundredth.**

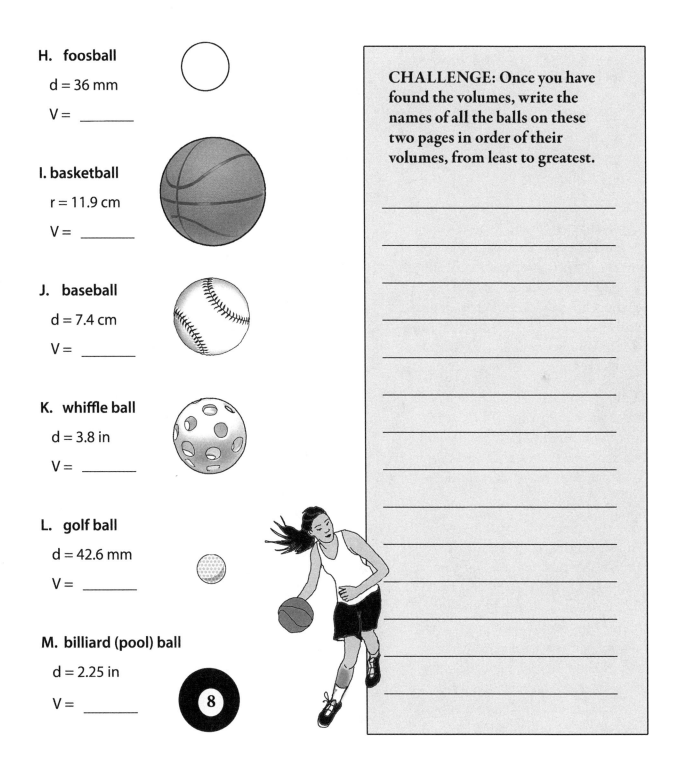

H. foosball

d = 36 mm

V = _____

I. basketball

r = 11.9 cm

V = _____

J. baseball

d = 7.4 cm

V = _____

K. whiffle ball

d = 3.8 in

V = _____

L. golf ball

d = 42.6 mm

V = _____

M. billiard (pool) ball

d = 2.25 in

V = _____

CHALLENGE: Once you have found the volumes, write the names of all the balls on these two pages in order of their volumes, from least to greatest.

Name

Use with page 108.

SPEAKING OF VOLUMES

Investigate some volumes related to the sports at a middle school.

Solve each of the volume problems to answer the question.

1. Each cheerleader at Central Middle School has a 15-inch-tall megaphone with a 3.5-inch radius to help magnify the volume of his or her voice. In terms of π, what is the volume of air that each megaphone can hold?

2. Lucy and Lamar each bring a cylindrical can of snacks to cricket practice. Lucy's can of chips has a radius of 4 centimeters and a height of 20 centimeters. Lamar's can of maple granola has a radius of 5 centimeters and a height of 12.8 centimeters. How do the volumes of their cans compare?

3. Three tennis balls in a can each have a diameter of 3 inches. The can has an interior diameter of 3 inches and a height of 9 inches. Using 3.14 for π, how much wasted space is inside the can?

4. Alex (suffering from "tennis elbow") finds a spherical container of pain-relieving cream for $5.50 and a cylindrical container with similar ingredients for the same price. The cylindrical jar has a 6-centimeter radius and a 10-centimeter height. The spherical container has a radius of 6.5 centimeters. Assuming that both containers are full, which is the better deal?

5. Hudson and Hannah each have a container of Choco-Melts in their athletic bag. Each candy has a volume of 0.15 cubic centimeters. Hudson's full container is a cylinder with an 8-centimeter height and a 3-centimeter radius. Hannah's full container is a cone with a 12-centimeter height and a 4-centimeter radius. Whose container holds more Choco-Melts, and approximately how many more?

6. The school athletic department owns 25 plastic cones used for various sports activities. Each cone is 45 centimeters tall and has a volume of 6,782.4 cubic centimeters. A closet measuring 2 meters wide by 2 meters long by 2.5 meters tall is used to store the cones. For some unknown reason, the coach likes to store the cones without stacking them. Can all 25 cones fit in this closet—unstacked?

7. The cylindrical water cooler at Samantha's soccer game has a 30-centimeter diameter and a 60-centimeter height. It is full of water. Samantha drops her 22-centimeter-diameter soccer ball into the cooler and puts the top on so that the ball is completely submerged. In terms of π, what is the volume of the water left in the cooler (rounded to the nearest whole cubic centimeter)?

Name

     Copyright © 2014 World Book, Inc./ Incentive Publications, Chicago, IL

STATISTICS AND PROBABILITY

Grade 8

I slide to bases with
relative frequency!

CLIMBING CONNECTIONS

These scatter plots were drawn to show some data about a climbing league's competitors and competitions. Climbing league members investigated different sets of variables for connections among data.

Examine and analyze the scatter plots. Above each one, write the letter of the description that best fits the plot:
 a. strong positive correlation
 b. strong negative correlation
 c. weak negative correlation
 d. correlation approximately zero
   (no linear correlation)

1

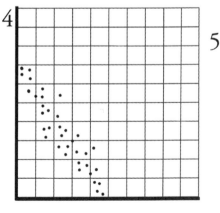

2

3
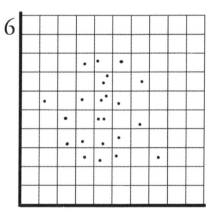

4

5
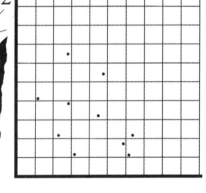

6
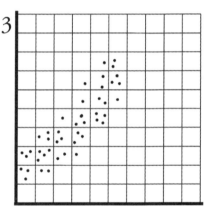

Name

A LONG HISTORY OF LONG JUMPS

The long jump for men has been a part of the modern Olympic Games since they began in 1896. The data on the table show the winning men's long-jump distances for several years of the Summer Olympic Games. You'll see an interruption in the sequence on the table below because World War I (1914-1918) caused the cancellation of the 1916 summer games.

Construct a scatter plot and investigate the data as directed.

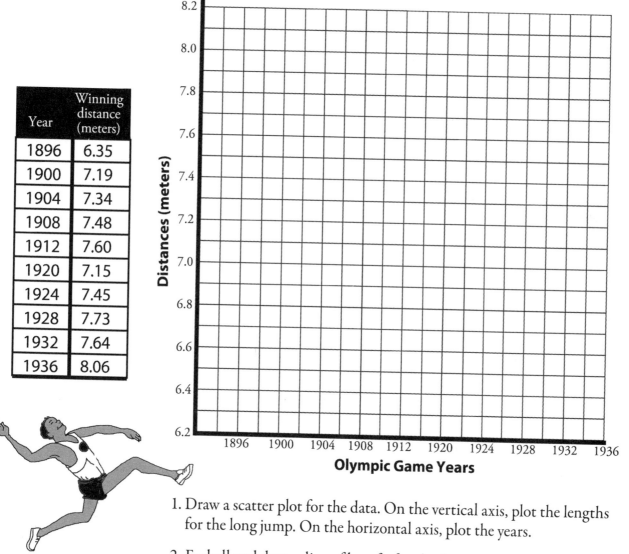

Year	Winning distance (meters)
1896	6.35
1900	7.19
1904	7.34
1908	7.48
1912	7.60
1920	7.15
1924	7.45
1928	7.73
1932	7.64
1936	8.06

1. Draw a scatter plot for the data. On the vertical axis, plot the lengths for the long jump. On the horizontal axis, plot the years.

2. Eyeball and draw a line of best fit for the data.

3. Is this statement true or false?
   The 1896 jump appears to be an outlier.

4. Is this statement true or false?
   In general, the winning long jump distance in the Olympics increased between 1896 and 1936.

Name

TEAM STATS

Investigate and analyze patterns in baseball stats (short for *statistics*) for some teams with memorable names. Continue the same work on page 115.

The data on the table show the batting averages and proportion of games won for nine baseball teams. Construct a scatter plot and investigate the data as directed in each step.

Team	Team Batting Average	Proportion of Games Won
Bombers	.283	.543
Tarantulas	.274	.562
Boomers	.268	.537
Black Sox	.263	.560
Striped Sox	.261	.528
No Sox	.261	.463
Great Lakes	.259	.481
Great Legs	.257	.522
Grizzlies	.257	.422

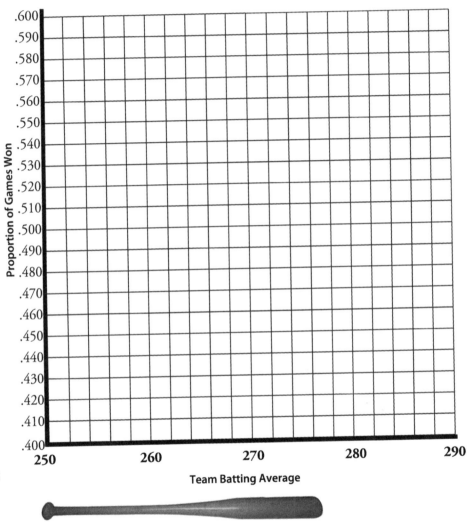

1. Draw a scatter plot for the data. On the vertical axis, plot the data for the proportion of games won. On the horizontal axis, plot the data for team batting averages.

2. Eyeball and draw a line of best fit for the data.

3. Which does the scatter plot show?

   a. There is a weak negative correlation for the variables.

   b. There is a weak positive correlation for the variables.

   c. There is a strong positive correlation for the variables.

   d. There is a strong negative correlation for the variables.

Use with page 115.

Name

The data on the table show the team earned-run averages (ERA) and proportion of games won for the same nine baseball teams as in the problems on the preceding page.

Construct a scatter plot and investigate the data as directed in each step.

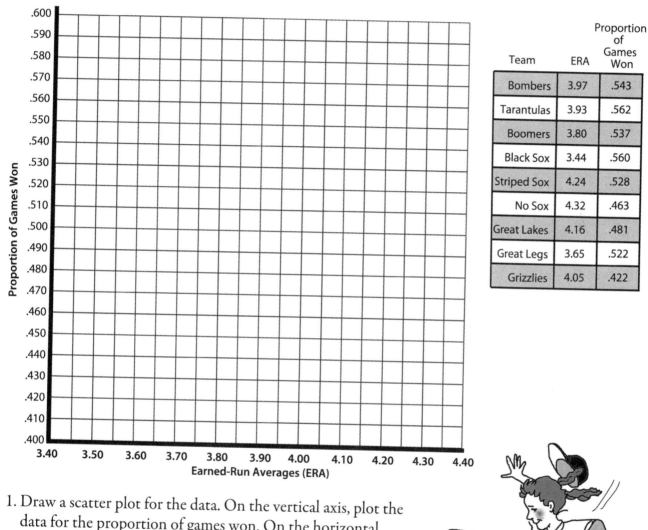

Team	ERA	Proportion of Games Won
Bombers	3.97	.543
Tarantulas	3.93	.562
Boomers	3.80	.537
Black Sox	3.44	.560
Striped Sox	4.24	.528
No Sox	4.32	.463
Great Lakes	4.16	.481
Great Legs	3.65	.522
Grizzlies	4.05	.422

1. Draw a scatter plot for the data. On the vertical axis, plot the data for the proportion of games won. On the horizontal axis, plot the data for earned-run averages.

2. Eyeball and draw a line of best fit for the data.

3. Which best describes the line?

   a. There is no straight line that approximates the data.

   b. There is a positive correlation between the variables.

   c. There is a negative correlation between the data.

   d. There is a nonlinear correlation between the data.

Name

Use with page 114.

READ THE DOTS

At an arm-wrestling tournament, Julie interviewed ten competitors about the numbers of arm and shoulder sprains, strains, or bruises so far this year. She also asked each one how many times he or she had competed during the year up to this competition. She summarized her data on a scatter plot. Notice that a line of best fit is drawn on the plot.

Analyze Julie's plot and the remainder of the plots on this page and page 117.

1.

On Julie's graph, what is represented by the line's y-intercept?

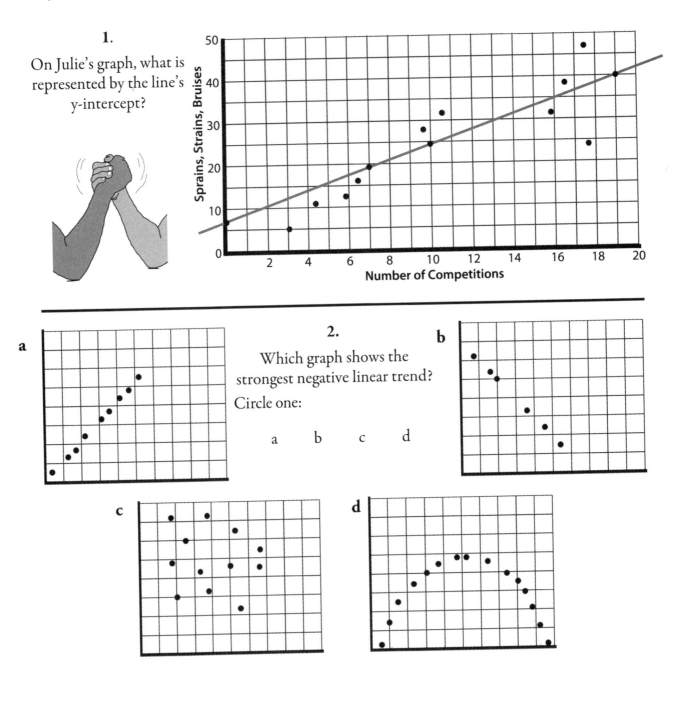

2.

Which graph shows the strongest negative linear trend?

Circle one:

a   b   c   d

Name

Analyze plots a, b, c, d, e, f, and g, and answer the questions below.

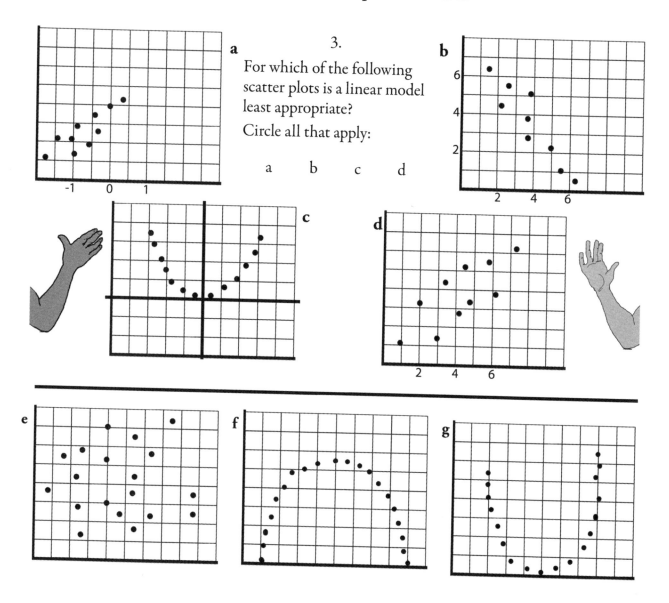

3.
For which of the following scatter plots is a linear model least appropriate?
Circle all that apply:

a   b   c   d

4. In plots e, f, and g above, the correlation is approximately _____.

5. True or false? **This means that there is no good straight line that approximates the data.**

6. True or false? **In f and g, there appears to be a nonlinear correlation.**

7. In f and g, what kind of function best approximates the data?

Name

Use with page 116.

SOME FISHY STATISTICS

Clear Lake, a pristine mountain lake, is a favorite fishing spot for Dan's family and many other fishing enthusiasts. Natural resource officials measured the average length of the fish in Clear Lake for fish of different ages. The table shows the data collected.

Follow the directions to investigate the data and construct a scatter plot.

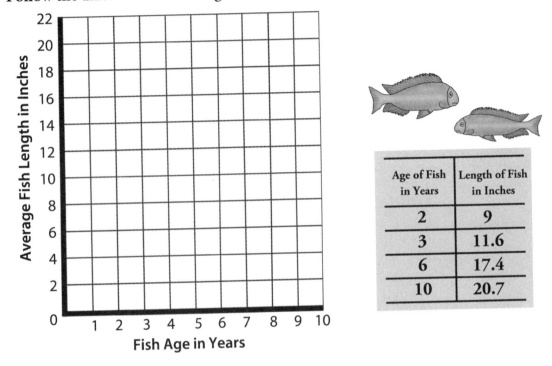

Age of Fish in Years	Length of Fish in Inches
2	9
3	11.6
6	17.4
10	20.7

1. Draw a scatter plot for the data. On the vertical axis, plot the data for the average fish length. On the horizontal axis, plot the data for the ages of the fish.

2. Try to eyeball a line of best fit for the data. Can you do this?

3. Give a reason for not expecting a linear relationship between average age and length of the fish.

4. Since Dan lives near Clear Lake, he fishes twice a week. For a long time, he's had good luck catching fish. But lately, that luck has changed. Dan creates a graph to correlate the decline in number of fish caught (y) with the number of weeks since he started to keep track of these numbers (x). These are two points on the line of his graph (1, 5) and (3, 9).

What is the rate of the decline in number of fish per week?

Name

AN EXPLOSIVE RECORD

David "The Bullet" Smith, Jr., set a world record for the longest distance a human was shot from a cannon. He traveled 59.05 meters with a speed, at the initial burst, of 120 kilometers per hour.

Follow the directions to consider how Mr. Smith's flight could be represented and to investigate the data shown on the graph.

The graph shows how the number of attempts at firing the cannon is related to the number of additional pounds of gunpowder brought in for the firings.

1. What is the meaning of the y-intercept on this graph?

2. What is the rate of change?

3. What is the equation for this line?

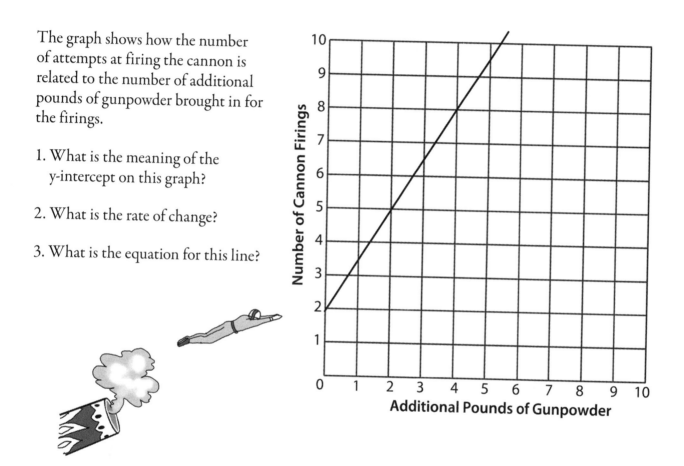

4. If a table gave the distance from the muzzle of the cannon and the height above the ground at given times of Mr. Smith's flight, would you expect to be able to get a straight line to best fit from the plotted data?

5. What kind of plot would be likely to fit these data best?

Name

JOGGING DATA

As a runner, Caitlin spends a lot of time at the track. Almost every day, even beyond competition season, she jogs laps around a track. She tries to keep a steady pace.

The table shows some data for one of Caitlin's recent jogs at the track.

Number of Laps	2	4	6	8	10	12	15
Time (min, sec)	3:10	6:40	10:20	13:30	16:40	20:09	25:44

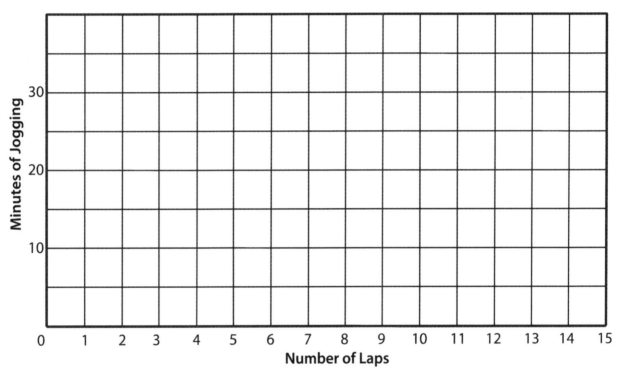

1. Draw a scatter plot for the data. On the vertical axis, plot time jogged. On the horizontal axis, plot the number of laps.

2. Eyeball a line of best fit for the data. Draw this line.

3. What does the slope of this line represent?

4. What does the y-intercept represent?

5. Did Caitlin keep a steady pace?

Name

TOURNAMENTS AND TESTS

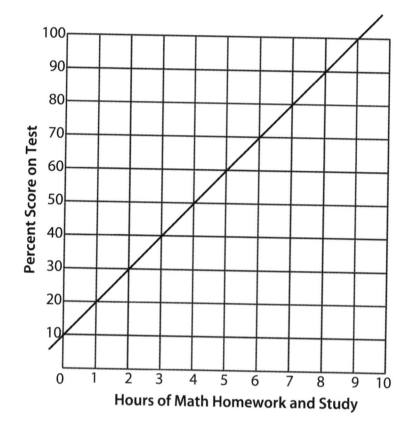

Jemma's soccer team is headed for the state finals. The team is practicing overtime, and the excitement is high throughout the school. Many of the team members are having a hard time focusing on homework and studying. Jemma has a big mathematics test the day before the team leaves for the championship tournament. The teacher encourages students to keep up with their homework and to study ahead of time for the test.

Before the test, the teacher asks students to calculate the number of hours they had spent on mathematics homework and test preparation in the three weeks before the test. Then she compares those data to the test scores. Here is a graph of the results.

Use the data on the graph to answer the questions.

1. If Jemma had wanted at least an 85% on her test, how many hours should she have spent on homework and study?

2. What test score could Jemma have expected if she had done no homework or test preparation? How do you know?

3. What is the equation for this line?

4. Describe the rate of change for this graph and what it meant for test scores.

Name _____

Common Core Reinforcement Activities — 8th Grade Math

HOOPS, HEIGHTS, AND FEET

Here are some data about the heights and shoe sizes of the players on the Rocky Point High School boys' basketball team. How are these data related?

The table shows the shoe size and heights for each player. Construct a data plot and investigate the data as directed in each step.

Height in Inches	Shoe Size
70	$10\frac{1}{2}$
73	$9\frac{1}{2}$
68	8
69	10
72	10
68	9
74	12
71	12
69	9
66	$8\frac{1}{2}$
71	9
70	10
73	$11\frac{1}{2}$

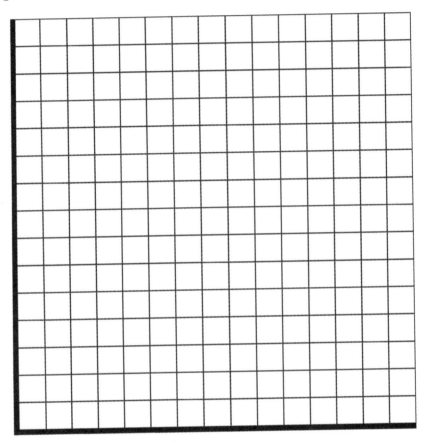

1. Draw a scatter plot for the data. Label and number the graph. On the vertical axis, plot the data for the shoe sizes. On the horizontal axis, plot the data for the heights.

2. Eyeball and draw a line of best fit for the data.

3. What does the slope of this line mean?

4. Does it make sense to extend the line far to the left?

Name

A GREAT RIVALRY

Two nearby high schools have a long-standing basketball rivalry.
Tables of data present some information about this rivalry.

Use the tables to examine, interpret, and display the data.

1. The Sparta Spartans and the Tomah Timberwolves play each
   other twice a year. This table shows win records in relationship
   to where the game was played over a period of several years.

Home Team	Sparta Won	Tomah Won
Sparta	33	22
Tomah	24	10

1. Is there a home court advantage? Use the data to decide.

   a. The team at home is more likely to win.

   b. It does not matter where the game is played.

   c. The team at home is less likely to win.

2. One of the team captains is so intent on helping his team succeed over its rival that, in addition
   to regular team practices, he spends an hour or more in rigorous physical training. Some days are
   harder than others. He suspects that weekend days are easier than the weekdays. To examine his
   suspicion about the relative difficulty of the days, he started to keep track. He noted that he felt
   lethargic and sick on 6 of 36 weekend days and 35 of 180 weekdays. On the other days, he felt
   quite energetic. Complete the following table with these data.

	% of days he felt sick	% of days he felt energetic
Weekend days		
Weekdays		

3. What conclusion should the captain draw from the data?

   a. He is most likely to feel sick on weekend days.

   b. He is least likely to feel sick on weekdays.

   c. He feels sick at about the same rate on weekdays or weekend days.

Name

Common Core Reinforcement Activities — 8th Grade Math

KEEPING UP THE GRADES

Athletics and academics have a special connection in middle school, high school, and college. In order to participate in their sports, athletes must maintain a respectable academic record. 100% of the students in Ms. Parabola's third-period algebra class are involved in some kind of school sport that requires students to maintain a B-average to remain active in the sport. So every test is important for the students' athletic participation.

The table below gives the frequencies of the particular range of scores on an English test taken by all members of the freshman class. Calculate the relative frequency for each of these ranges. Round the frequencies to the nearest hundredth. Use the completed table to answer questions 9, 10, and 11. Then solve problem 12.

	Test Score Range	Frequency	Relative Frequency
1	$20 < x \le 30$	2	
2	$30 < x \le 40$	0	
3	$40 < x \le 50$	3	
4	$50 < x \le 60$	5	
5	$60 < x \le 70$	20	
6	$70 < x \le 80$	42	
7	$80 < x \le 90$	30	
8	$90 < x \le 100$	18	

9. Are there any outliers? If so, what are they?

10. Do the relative frequencies add up to one (equivalent to 100%)?

11. True or false? **Relative frequency indicates a percent while frequency indicates a count.**

12. Jake and Jill are brother and sister. Over time, in 2,240 rounds of golf, Jill's score was 165 times below par. Her brother scored under par 180 times over 4,557 rounds. Based on their past performances, which sibling is more likely to score under par?

Name

CAFFEINE AND CHESS

Explore relative frequencies to solve problems on these two topics.

Answer the questions that follow each problem.

Alicia surveyed classmates at her school to examine possible connections between caffeine intake and sleepiness during classes. She asked 463 students whether they had consumed highly caffeinated drinks before school during the past week. She also asked them if they had fallen asleep in class during the day. The table shows data from her survey.

	Fell asleep in class	Did not fall asleep in class
Drank a caffeinated beverage every day	11	102
Drank a caffeinated beverage sometimes	84	120
Never drank a caffeinated beverage	66	80

1. What percent of students who drink caffeinated drinks daily fall asleep in class?

   a. not enough information to answer   b. 10%   c. 15%

2. Which of the following best describes the relationship between sleepiness in class and consumption of caffeinated drinks before school?

   a. There is no relationship between falling asleep in class and drinking caffeinated beverages.

   b. Students who drink caffeinated beverages are equally likely to fall asleep as those who don't.

   c. The more often students drink caffeinated beverages, the less likely they are to fall asleep.

   d. Students who drink caffeinated beverages are more likely to fall asleep in class.

Anne and Jesse are chess players. Over the past year, Anne has won 33% of her games whereas Jesse has won 47% of hers. Between the two, they played 575 games last year.

3. What % of their total games were won?

    a. 40%   b. 42%   c. not enough information

4. What conclusion about their chess playing is most reasonable?

   a. Anne is more likely to win a chess game than Jesse.

   b. Jesse is more likely to win a chess game than Anne.

   c. They are equally likely to win.

   d. There is not enough information to answer.

Name

A WORTHY REQUIREMENT?

Should physical education be a requirement for all students in middle schools and high schools? Two students decided to learn their classmates' and teachers' opinions about this question, so they got busy taking samples and conducting interviews.

Use the tables below to answer the questions.

	% who said yes	% who said no
Students		
Teachers		

Jackson asked a random sample of classmates and teachers in his school the question of whether or not physical education should be a requirement. 60 students said yes, whereas 80 said no. 15 teachers said yes, and 14 said no.

1. Complete the above table, rounding to the nearest whole percent.

2. What could Jackson report about the opinions at his school on the PE requirement?

   a. A larger percent of students than teachers supported the PE requirement.

   b. A larger percent of teachers than students supported the PE requirement.

Nina interviewed all the students in her study hall. This included students who participated in some school sports and students who did not. She asked each student if he or she believed that physical education should be required of all students at the school. The table shows her results.

	# who said yes	# who said no
Out for sports	21	22
Not out for sports	24	11

3. Which of the following is the best conclusion from the data?

   a. There is no relationship between these variables.

   b. Students out for sports think PE should be required more than students who are not out for sports.

   c. Students not out for sports think PE should be required more than students who are out for sports.

Name

ASSESSMENT AND ANSWER KEYS

This is one test
I can ace!

MATH ASSESSMENT

PART ONE: THE NUMBER SYSTEM

Do not use a calculator for this page.

Write T (true) or F (false).

_____ 1. All repeating decimals are irrational numbers.

_____ 2. Any fraction with a radical in the denominator is irrational.

_____ 3. Any multiple of π is irrational.

_____ 4. The decimal expansion of an irrational number never repeats or terminates.

_____ 5. The sum of two rational numbers is a rational number.

6. Circle letters of golf balls with irrational numbers.

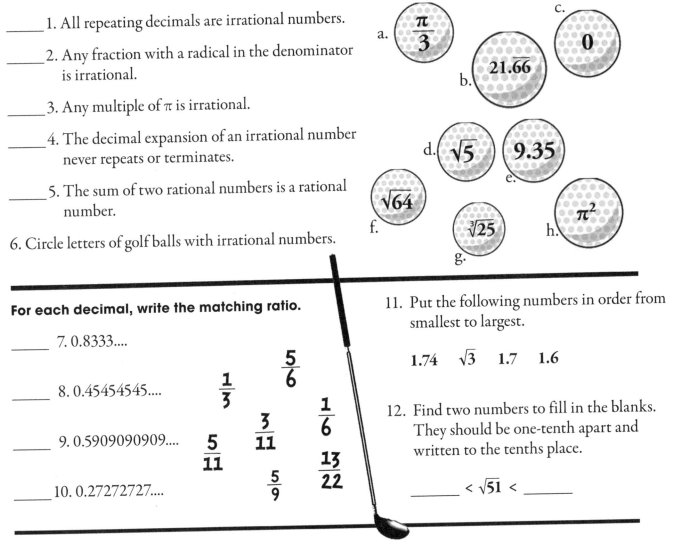

For each decimal, write the matching ratio.

_____ 7. 0.8333....

_____ 8. 0.45454545....

_____ 9. 0.5909090909....

_____ 10. 0.27272727....

$\frac{5}{6}$ $\frac{1}{3}$ $\frac{1}{6}$ $\frac{3}{11}$ $\frac{5}{11}$ $\frac{13}{22}$ $\frac{5}{9}$

11. Put the following numbers in order from smallest to largest.

    1.74 $\sqrt{3}$ **1.7**   **1.6**

12. Find two numbers to fill in the blanks. They should be one-tenth apart and written to the tenths place.

    _____ $< \sqrt{51} <$ _____

13. When Savannah walked to the green, she found that her golf ball landed a distance (in meters) from the hole at a measurement close to the value of $\sqrt{33}$. Which point (A or B) more closely represents this distance?

PART TWO: EXPRESSIONS AND EQUATIONS

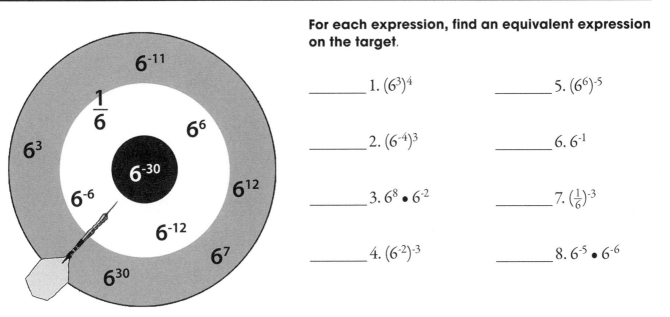

For each expression, find an equivalent expression on the target.

_____ 1. $(6^3)^4$

_____ 5. $(6^6)^{-5}$

_____ 2. $(6^{-4})^3$

_____ 6. 6^{-1}

_____ 3. $6^8 \cdot 6^{-2}$

_____ 7. $\left(\frac{1}{6}\right)^{-3}$

_____ 4. $(6^{-2})^{-3}$

_____ 8. $6^{-5} \cdot 6^{-6}$

Find the value of each expression.

_____ 9. $\left(\frac{2}{6}\right)^{-2} =$

_____ 12. $(-5)^3 =$

_____ 10. $8^{-2} =$

_____ 13. $(-4)^{-3} =$

_____ 11. $\left(\frac{1}{2}\right)^{-5} =$

_____ 14. $7^3 \cdot 7^{-1} =$

Circle one answer for 15-18.

15. The value of 5^{-4} is
    less than -1
    between 0 and 1
    equal to 1
    greater than 1

16. The value of $\frac{7^{-5}}{7^{-5}}$ is
    less than -1
    between 0 and 1
    equal to 1
    greater than 1

17. The value of -10^{-5} is
    less than -1
    between 0 and 1
    equal to 1
    greater than 1

18. In an afternoon of practice, archer Anya scored 224 points. Which expression most closely represents this number?

    a. 15^2 b. $6^3 + 2^3$ c. $83 - 17^2$

Answer the questions.

19. The number of archery ranges in Anya's county is $\sqrt[3]{5,832}$. The number of ranges in her state is $\sqrt{4,489}$. How many more ranges are in the state than in her county?

20. In 1998, Denise Parker, of the United States, became the youngest archer to win an Olympic medal. Her age at the time was $\sqrt{196}$ years. What was her age?

Name

Write these masses in standard notation.

21. The mass of a bus carrying archers to a competition: 1.63×10^4 kilograms

22. The mass of the feather on the archer's bow: 4.5×10^{-3} kilograms

Write these numbers in scientific notation.

23. 0.000077

24. 62,350,000,000,000

25. 0.00000894

Solve the problems.
Write the answers in scientific notation.

26. $(5.3 \times 10^3)\,(6.0 \times 10^{-6}) =$

27. $(7.1)\,(7 \times 10^4) =$

28. $\dfrac{(9.5 \times 10^{-5})\,(4.0 \times 10^9)}{9.5 \times 10^{-2}} =$

29. Circle perfect squares or cubes on the target.

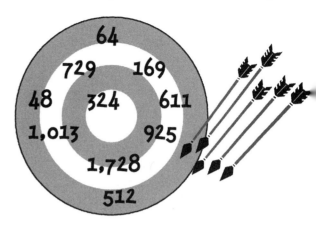

Use these equations for problems 30-32.
   a. $5b = -4b + 9b$
   b. $-4x - 4 = 4x$
   c. $-x = -x - 8$
   d. $-8x + 7x = -x$

Which equation or equations have . . .

30. one solution?

31. infinitely many solutions?

32. no solutions?

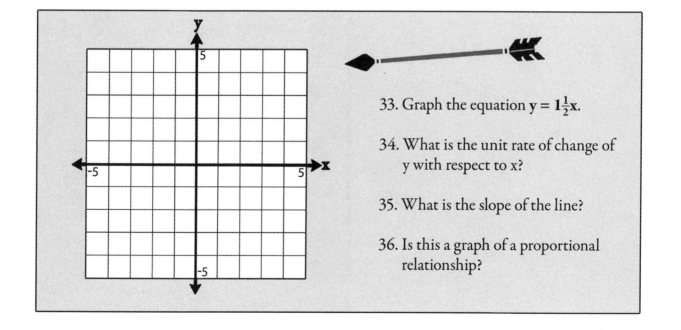

33. Graph the equation $y = 1\frac{1}{2}x$.

34. What is the unit rate of change of y with respect to x?

35. What is the slope of the line?

36. Is this a graph of a proportional relationship?

Name

Write the missing term.

Let x = -5.

37. $2(2x - 5) +$ _____ = -10

38. $3x(1 + 2) +$ _____ $- 18 = -1$

Circle one answer.

39. The solution is x = 5.
What is the equation?

   a. $x - 5 + 4x = -20$

   b. $x + 7 - 4x = -8$

   c. $2(x + 9) = x + 3$

   d. $\frac{5x}{3} + x = 8x - 10$

40. How many solutions exist for the system of equations?

$$x - 2y = 2$$
$$2x = 4y + 4$$

   a. one solution

   b. no solutions

   c. infinitely many solutions

Circle one answer.

44. Graph **a** has:

   a. one solution

   b. no solutions

   c. infinitely many solutions

45. Graph **b** has:

   a. one solution

   b. no solutions

   c. infinitely many solutions

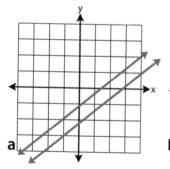

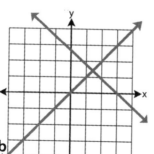

Circle one answer.

41. Which of the following choices of **b** will result in a system of linear equations with infinitely many solutions?

$$-x + 3y = -4$$
$$x - 3y = b$$

Solve for x and y.

42. $y = 3x - 2$

   $y = -x - 6$

43. $3x + 10 = 5y$

   $7x + 20 = -5y$

Solve each age problem.

46. Lucy is half the age of her sister Mazie. In two years, the sum of their ages will be 28. How old is Mazie?

47. In 21 years, archer Nan will be four times as old as she is today. What is her age today?

48. Lance and Caden are teammates. The sum of their ages is 30. In 10 years, Lance, the older, will be 4 years more than twice Caden's age now. What are their ages now?

Name

PART THREE: FUNCTIONS

Answer the questions about functions.

1. Something unusual happened at the high school basketball game tonight. Every time the Panthers increased their score, the Cougars came right back with double the points. When Jamie sunk 1 free throw, the Cougars scored a 2-point basket. When Sam hit a 2-point basket, the Cougars got 4 points within seconds. When Lou hit a 3-point basket, the Cougars sank two 3-pointers in a row.

   Does this situation represent a function?

2. Could the following coordinate pairs represent a function?

   $(2, -2)$ $(4, 3)$ $(5, 7)$ $(2, 0)$

3. In the formula $A = lw$, is A a function of l?

4. Does $x = 4$ represent y as a function of x?

5. Is $f(x) = x + 5$ a function?

6. Which table represents a function?

   p   q   both   neither

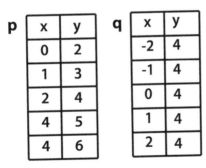

p	x	y
	0	2
	1	3
	2	4
	4	5
	4	6

q	x	y
	-2	4
	-1	4
	0	4
	1	4
	2	4

Use the graphs below for 7-10

7. Which graphs below represent a function?

8. What is the equation of graph **a**?

9. Is graph **d** a graph of **x** as a function of **y**?

10. What is the equation of graph **f**?

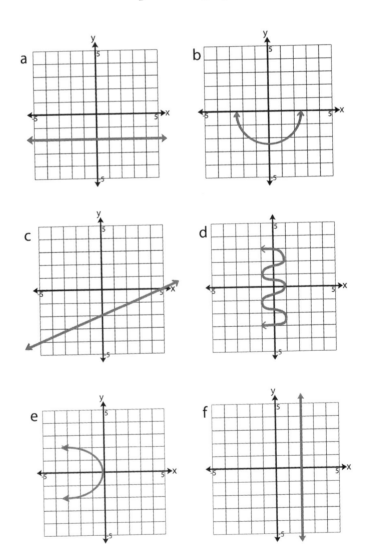

For 11-20, follow the directions in each problem.

11. Basketball player Michelle (y) is 12 years less than 4 times the age of her sister (x), who is learning to play basketball.

    a. What is the equation for this sentence?

    b. Does the sentence describe a linear function?

12. Does the table represent a linear relationship? Explain your answer.

x	y
1	5
4	10
7	15
10	16
13	17

13. Given a point (-3, 4) and the slope -3, write the equation of the line in slope-intercept form.

14. What is the slope of a line through the points (5, 4) and (-3, -1)?

15. Given the line $y = mx + b$, what is the y-intercept?

16. What is the x-intercept of $3y + 2x = 6$?

17. Find the slope of $\frac{5}{x+y} = \frac{2}{x}$

18. Find the equation of the line with slope -2 and through point (-2, 5).

19. Which function corresponds to the graph?

    a. $y = \frac{1}{2}x$ d. $y = \frac{1}{2}x - 1$

    b. $y = 2x - 1$ e. $y = 1 - \frac{1}{2}x$

    c. $y = \frac{1}{2}x + 1$ f. none of these

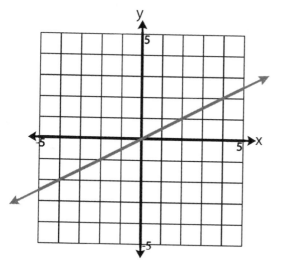

20. Graph the function $y = 3x - 3$.

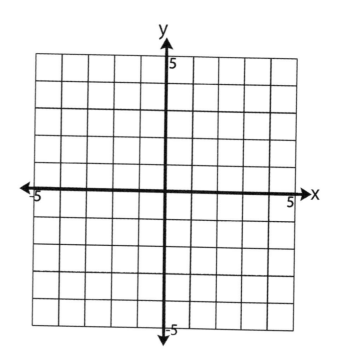

Name

Common Core Reinforcement Activities — 8th Grade Math

PART FOUR: GEOMETRY

Answer the questions.

1. Quadrilateral A is reflected across a line. How does the sum of the angles in the reflected figure compare to the sum of the angles in A?

2. When an angle is translated on a graph -6 in relation to the x-axis and +4 in relation to the y-axis, what happens to its measurement?

3. Two sides of triangle LMN measure 5 centimeters each. The angle between them is 60°. The corresponding sides and angle of triangle XYZ have the same measurements. Are the two triangles congruent?

4. Two parallel lines are rotated -90° around the origin on a graph. What is the resulting figure?

5. (-3, -2) is a point on line **g**. What is the new location of the point when **g** is translated +3 in relation to the x-axis and -6 in relation to the y-axis?

6. Line segment **b** has endpoints (2, 5) and (4, 2). In what quadrants will this lie after it is reflected across the y-axis?

7. The vertex of angle PQR is located at (-7, -4) on a graph. When the figure is rotated 270° around its axis, what will be the location of its axis?

Use graphs A, B, C, D for problems 8-11.

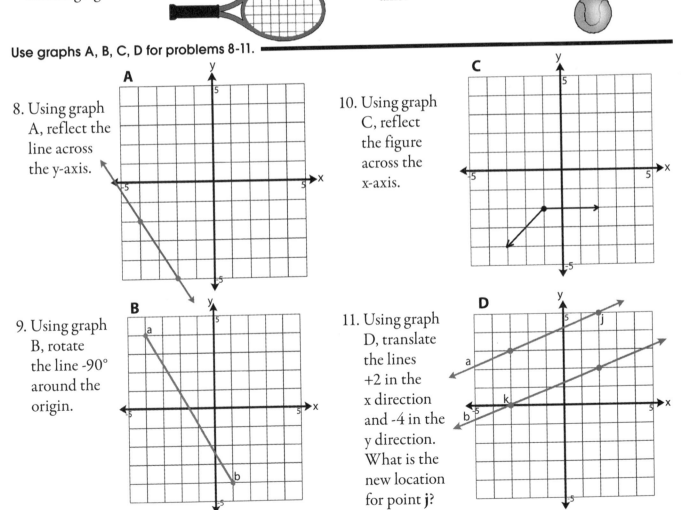

8. Using graph A, reflect the line across the y-axis.

9. Using graph B, rotate the line -90° around the origin.

10. Using graph C, reflect the figure across the x-axis.

11. Using graph D, translate the lines +2 in the x direction and -4 in the y direction. What is the new location for point **j**?

Name

Answer the questions.

12. A figure has vertices at P (-4, 1), Q (-3, -2), and R (-4, -5). After reflection across x = -1, what is the location of R_1?

13. Point T is located at (-8, -6). When translated +10 in relation to the x-axis and -3 in relation to the y-axis, what is the location of T_1?

14. A figure has vertices at A (-4, -1), B (1, 3), and C (0, -5). After a scale change of 0.5, where is point A_1?

15. A figure has vertices at D (-4, -1), E (1, 3), F (3, 0), and G (0, -5). When rotated 180°, where will point F_1 be located?

16. A volleyball court is a 60-foot long and 30-foot wide rectangle. Halley practices on a rectangular surface that is 40 feet long and 20 feet wide. Are these surfaces similar figures?

17. Lines a and b are parallel. Which angles are congruent to angle 5?

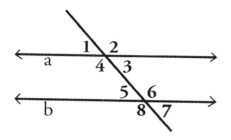

Use the figure below for 18-20.

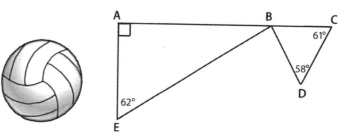

18. What is the measure of ∠ ABC?

19. What is the measure of ∠ EBD?

20. What is the measure of ∠ EBA?

21. On graph **A**, reflect the figure across the line **y = -1**. What is the new location for point **p**?

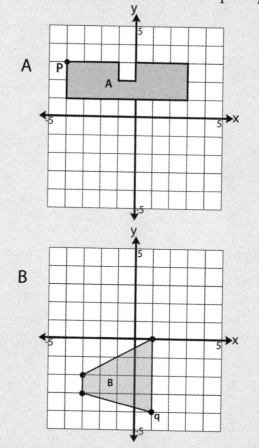

22. On graph B, translate figure B -2 in relation to the x-axis and +4 in relation to the y-axis. What is the new location for point **q**?

Name

Common Core Reinforcement Activities — 8th Grade Math

Math Assessment

Answer the questions.

23. Some friends are practicing baseball on fields A and B. Are these fields congruent? Explain your answer.

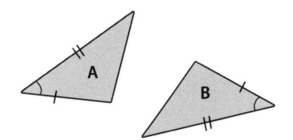

24. What is the missing side measurement?

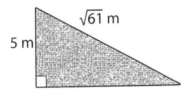

√61 m

5 m

25. What is the missing side measurement?

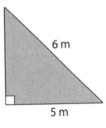

6 m

5 m

26. Todd throws the ball straight to Kate who throws the ball straight to Sue. Sue throws it to Kate who throws it back to Todd, who throws it to Sue. How far does the ball travel?

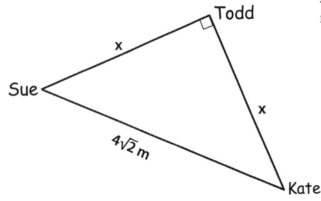

Todd

x

Sue

x

4√2 m

Kate

27. Which has the greater volume: the megaphone or the basketball?

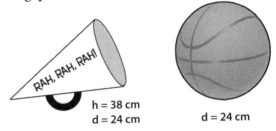

RAH, RAH, RAH!

h = 38 cm
d = 24 cm

d = 24 cm

28. Will's pre-game energy drink is in a cylindrical can that is 12 centimeters tall, with a volume of 108π cubic centimeters. What is the can's diameter?

29. Alexis takes a cylindrical bucket of softballs out to the field to practice hitting. Each softball has a 9-centimeter diameter. The bucket is 46 centimeters tall and has a diameter of 30 centimeters. The volume of empty space in the bucket is 530 cubic centimeters. Approximately how many softballs are in the bucket?

30. After the game, 12 team members share a pizza. The pizza is sliced through the center into 12 equal wedges. The pizza is 2.5 inches thick and has a volume of 202.5π cubic inches. What is the long edge measurement of each pizza slice?

Name

PART FIVE: STATISTICS AND PROBABILITY

Above each scatter plot, write the letter of the description that best fits the plot.

a. strong positive correlation   c. weak negative correlation
b. strong negative correlation   d. correlation approximately zero

1. _____   2. _____   3. _____   4. _____   5. _____

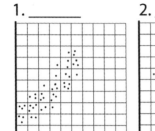 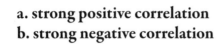 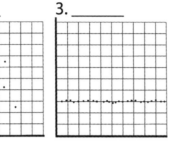 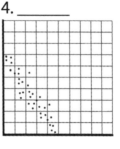 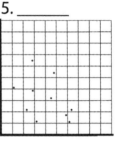

Use graph A for 6-9.

6. What is the slope?

7. What does the slope represent?

8. What does the y-intercept represent?

9. What kind of correlation is shown?

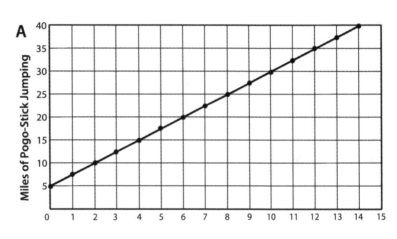

A — Miles of Pogo-Stick Jumping

Use graph B for 10-11.

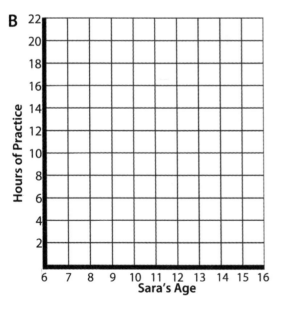

B — Hours of Practice / Sara's Age

10. The data on the table show how the number of hours Sara practiced pogo-stick jumping each week changed over a period of 8 years. Plot the data.

11. Try to eyeball a line of best fit. Is there a linear correlation? Give a possible explanation for this.

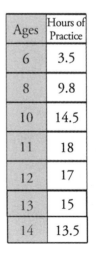

Ages	Hours of Practice
6	3.5
8	9.8
10	14.5
11	18
12	17
13	15
14	13.5

Name

Common Core Reinforcement Activities — 8th Grade Math

Use scatter plots a, b, c, d, and e to answer questions 12-15.

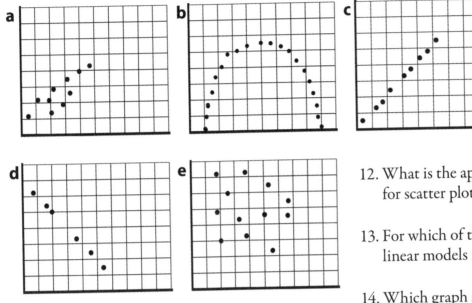

12. What is the approximate correlation for scatter plot **b**?

13. For which of the scatter plots are linear models most appropriate?

14. Which graph shows the strongest positive linear trend?

15. What kind of function best approximates the data on graph **b**?

Dana, an Xpogo (extreme pogo) athlete, interviewed all the athletes at a competition about whether they also participated in extreme snowboarding or skateboarding. The table shows the results of his survey.

16. Complete the table. Round the frequencies to the nearest hundredth.

17. Which conclusion is most reasonable from the data?

    a. Xpogo athletes are not likely to be skateboarders.

    b. Xpogo athletes are likely to also be extreme skateboarders or extreme snowboarders or both.

XPogo Competitors participated in	Frequency	Relative Frequency
Snowboarding	12	
Skateboarding	28	
Both	14	
Neither	2	

ASSESSMENT ANSWER KEY

Part One: The Number System

1. F
2. F
3. T
4. T
5. T
6. Circle: a, d, g, h
7. $\frac{5}{6}$
8. $\frac{5}{11}$
9. $\frac{13}{22}$
10. $\frac{3}{11}$
11. 1.6, 1.7, $\sqrt{3}$; 1.74
12. 7.1 and 7.2
13. b

Part Two: Expressions and Equations

1. 6^{12}
2. 6^{-12}
3. 6^6
4. 6^6
5. 6^{-30}
6. $\frac{1}{6}$
7. 6^3
8. 6^{-11}
9. $\frac{36}{4}$ or 9
10. $\frac{1}{64}$
11. 32
12. -125
13. $-\frac{1}{64}$
14. 49
15. between 0 and 1
16. equal to one
17. less than negative 1
18. b
19. 49
20. 14
21. 16,300
22. 0.0045
23. 7.7×10^{-5}
24. 6.235×10^{13}
25. 8.94×10^{-6}
26. 3.18×10^{-2}
27. 4.97×10^5
28. 4.0×10^6
29. 64, 169, 324, 512, 729, and 1,728
30. b
31. a and d
32. c
33. The line should include points (0, 0) and (2, 3).
34. $\frac{3}{2}$
35. $\frac{3}{2}$
36. yes
37. 20
38. 62
39. b
40. c
41. b
42. x = -1; y = -5
43. x = -3; y = $\frac{1}{5}$
44. b
45. a
46. 16
47. 7
48. Lance is 18; Caden is 12

Part Three: Functions

1. yes
2. no
3. yes
4. no
5. yes
6. q
7. a, b, and c
8. y = -2
9. no
10. x = 2
11. a. y = 4x – 12; b. yes
12. no; the graph is not a straight line
13. y = 3x – 5
14. $\frac{5}{8}$
15. b
16. x = 3
17. $\frac{3}{2}$
18. y = -2x + 1
19. a
20. The line should include points (0, -3) and (2, 3).

Part Four: Geometry

1. It stays the same.
2. It stays the same.
3. yes
4. two parallel lines
5. (0, -8)
6. quadrant II only
7. (-7, -4)
8. The reflected line will include these points: (4, -2) and (2, -5).
9. When the line is rotated, a_1 will be at (4, 4) and b_1 will be at (-4, -1)
10. Angle vertex will be at (-1, 2) with left leg passing through (-3, 4) and right leg passing through (1, 2).
11. Line a_1 will pass through points (-1, -1) and (4, 1). Line b_1 will pass through points (-1, -4) and (4, -2). Point j_1 is located at (4, 1).
12. (2, -5)
13. (2, -9)
14. (-2, -0.5)
15. (-3, 0)
16. yes
17. 1, 3, and 7
18. 180°
19. 91°
20. 28°
21. (-4, -5)
22. (-1, 0)
23. yes, side-angle-side rule
24. 6m
25. $\sqrt{11}$ m
26. $12 + 8\sqrt{2}$ m
27. basketball
28. 6 cm
29. 84
30. 9 inches

Part Five: Statistics and Probability

1. a
2. d
3. d
4. b
5. c
6. $\frac{5}{2}$
7. rate of change of the number of blisters per mile
8. zero blisters at 5 miles
9. steadily increasing positive correlation
10. Look for dots plotted to match the data. They will form somewhat of a line with a positive slope until age 12, where the line begins to fall to a negative slope.
11. There is no straight line to match the data. The dots show a positive correlation through age 11 but take a negative turn after that. Explanations will vary, but students might suggest such ideas as: Sara got too busy to practice as much due to more homework, began to lose interest in practicing, became injured and could not practice as much, or had polished her skills to the point where she did not need as much practice.
12. zero
13. a, c, and d
14. c
15. quadratic (or parabola)
16. snowboarding: 0.21; skateboarding: 0.5; both: 0.25; neither: 0.04
17. b

Common Core Reinforcement Activities — 8th Grade Math

ACTIVITIES ANSWER KEY

The Number System (pages 18-24)

page 18

Marilee's path will be:
First row: between $\sqrt{2}$ and $\sqrt{3}$
Second row: between π and $\sqrt{10}$
Third row: between $\sqrt{6}$ and $\frac{\pi}{2}$
Fourth row: between $\sqrt{7}$ and $\frac{3\pi}{2}$
Fifth row: between $\sqrt{5}$ and $\sqrt{8}$

page 19

1. T	6. T	11. F
2. T	7. F	12. T
3. F	8. F	13. F
4. T	9. F	14. F
5. T	10. T	

pages 20-21

On page 20, shirts b, c, e, g, h, i, k, and l should be shaded red. Shirts a, d, f, and j are with the wrong team. They should be circled and shaded blue.

On page 21, n, q, s, t, w, and x should be shaded blue. Shirts m, o, p, r, u, and v are with the wrong team. They should be shaded red.

page 22

1. f
2. b
3. The definition needs an additional phrase "and b ≠ 0"
4. $\frac{1}{3}$
5. $\frac{3}{11}$
6. $\frac{1}{6}$
7. $\frac{5}{6}$
8. $\frac{5}{9}$
9. $\frac{13}{22}$
10. $\frac{5}{11}$

page 23

1. 4; 4.12; $\sqrt{17}$; 4.2
2. 2; 2.4; $\sqrt{6}$; 3
3. 1.5; 1.7; $\sqrt{3}$; 1.74
4. 3; $\sqrt{10}$; 3.163; 3.2
5. 2.6; 2.61; $\sqrt{7}$; 2.65
6. 4.6; $\sqrt{23}$; 4.8; 4.9
7. $\sqrt{31}$; 5.6; 5.61; 5.7

8. 6.5; $\sqrt{43}$; 6.6; $\sqrt{49}$

pages 24-25

1. B	5. A
2. A	6. B
3. B	7. A
4. B	8. A

page 26

1. 5.1; 5.2
2. 5.5; 5.6
3. 6.7; 6.8
4. 4.3; 4.4
5. 2.6; 2.7
6. 7.1; 7.2
7. 3.6; 3.7
8. 6.24; 6.25

Expressions and Equations (pages 28-58)

page 28

A. 5^{24}	D. 5^{-15}
B. 5^{-32}	E. 5^9
C. 5^{35}	

1. 3	3. 10	5. 8	7. 3
2. 28	4. 36	6. -8	8. -2

page 29

1. less than -1
2. between 0 and 1
3. between 0 and 1
4. greater than 1
5. between 0 and 1
6. between 0 and 1
7. equal to 1
8. equal to 1
9. 8
10. 81
11. $\frac{1}{36}$
12. 32
13. 49
14. $\frac{5}{2}$
15. 9
16. 27
17. $\frac{1}{256}$
18. $\frac{512}{343}$

page 30

Here are the matching expressions.
1. 6^{-3}; $\frac{1}{216}$
2. 10^4; 10,000
3. 5^3; 125
4. -7^3; -343

5. $(-2)^6$; 64
6. 10^{-5}; $\frac{1}{100,000}$
7. 11^{-2}; $\frac{1}{121}$
8. 25^{-1}; $\frac{1}{25}$
9. 3^5; 243
10. $2^6 \cdot 2^{-8}$; $\frac{1}{4}$
11. $(-50)^2$; 2,500
12. $4^3 \cdot 4^{-1}$; 16

page 31

1. mistake: multiplying the exponents of two different numbers; correct answer is $7^{-16} \cdot 4^{80}$
2. mistake: subtracting the exponents instead of adding them; correct answer is 6^{-12}
3. mistake: multiplying the first two exponents (3 and -4) instead of adding them; correct answer is 5^{-2}
4. mistake: multiplying 4 and 6; adding all the exponents; correct answer is: $4^{12} \cdot 6^{-6}$
5. mistake: adding the exponents instead of subtracting them; correct answer is 9^{-7}
6. mistake: dividing the exponents instead of subtracting them; correct answer is 8^8
7. mistake: not using the inverse of the fraction before squaring; correct answer is $\frac{9}{16}$
8. mistake: keeping the negative; correct answer is $\frac{125}{8}$
9. mistake: not using the reciprocal before squaring; correct answer is $\frac{1}{36}$
10. mistake: keeping the negative on the answer; correct answer is 9

page 32

1. b
2. a
3. b
4. c
5. $\frac{1}{64}$

6. $5x^3$
7. $18n^5$
8. a^{-14}
9. $\frac{9}{16}$
10. -125

page 33

Trail follows these numbers, starting from the top and ending at the pizza: 64; 1,000; 256; 27; 343; 216; 125; 512; 196; 10,000; 144; 289; 729; 484; 900; 8,000; 121; 9

page 34

1. 18
2. 1,848
3. 5
4. 10
5. 4
6. 336
7. 67
8. 6

page 35

Number for the blank section: 66.

page 36

1. 1,700 kg
2. 72 kg
3. 0.000005 kg
4. 555 kg
5. 1,100 kg
6. 0.00000049 kg
7. 2.2×10^{-4} kg
8. 1.4×10^3 kg
9. 7.3477×10^{22} kg
10. 6.85×10^{-1} kg
11. 4.2×10^3 kg
12. 6.6×10^{-3}

page 37

Distances to be circled are: 8.8×10^4; 9.3×10^4; 2.1×10^4; 6.33×10^2; 9.35×10^3; and 3.625×10^5

page 38

1. $4.05 \times 10^5 - 3.6 \times 10^5$ $= 4.5 \times 10^4$ km
2. yes
3. The trip would take 70,000 years. Students should have an answer that is the difference between their age and 10 subtracted from 70,000.

4. $9.296 \times 10^7 - 2.572 \times 10^7 =$
   6.724×10^7 mi
5. 9.45×10^{15} m
6. yes
7. 3.0×10^{24}

page 39
1. $(2.5 \times 10^6)/(2.0 \times 10^5) =$
   1.25×10^1
2. $(1.82 \times 10^5)/(3.5 \times 10^{-1}) =$
   5.2×10^5
3. $(1.80 \times 10^5)/3.0 \times 10^{-5} =$
   6.0×10^9
4. 3.1×10^{-3}
5. 5.0×10^9
6. 2.2×10^4
7. 6.75×10^1
8. 1×10^{-2}
9. 2.0×10^3
10. 2.6×10^{-6}
11. 3.0×10^{-2}
12. 4.0×10^6

pages 40-41
1. The line should include points (0, 0) and (2, 3). Answer: a, b, c, d
2. The line should include points (0, 0) and (3, 4). Answer: a, b, c, d
3. The line should include points (0, 0) and (1, 2). The unit rate of change is 2.
4. The line should include the points (0, 0) and (3, 5). The equation is $y = \frac{5}{3}x$.
5. c

page 42
1. d
2. a
3. b

pages 43-45
1. a and b
2. a and d
3. A. $\frac{y+3}{x} = -2$
   B. $y = -2x - 3$
4. a and b
5.
   A. All right angles are equal.
   B. Corresponding angles of parallel lines are equal.
   C. Corresponding angles of parallel lines are equal.
   D. If corresponding

angles of two triangles are equal, then the triangles are similar.
   E. The ratios of corresponding sides of similar triangles are equal.
6. True

pages 46-47
Net A (one solution): 2, 6, 9; Net B (no solutions): 4, 5, 7; Net C (infinitely many solutions): 1, 3, 8, 10
Simplifications:
1. infinitely many solutions
2. one solution
3. infinitely many solutions
4. no solution
5. no solution
6. one solution
7. no solution
8. infinitely many solutions
9. one solution
10. infinitely many solutions
11. a
12. b
13. c
14. d
15. c
16. b

page 48
1. $b = 0$
2. $g = 4$
3. $m = 8$
4. 10
5. $x = 28$
6. $x = 4$
7. $x = -1$
8. $x = \frac{1}{3}$
9. $x = -\frac{17}{5}$
10. $x = 15$

page 49
Missing numbers and symbols are:
A. 20   E. -9
B. +   F. −
C. 10   G. 20
D. 6

page 50
1. 128
2. 81
3. 99
4. 141
5. b

6. b
7. c
8. c

page 51
$a = 4$; $b = 8$; $c = -5$;
$d = -1$; $e = 20$

page 52
1. 24
2. 31
3. 5
4. 16
5. 8
6. 18
7. Abby is 6; Jose is 16
8. 7
9. Savannah is 23; Mariah is 19
10. 13

page 53
1. a
2. c
3. c
4. b
5. c
6. b
7. c

pages 54-55
1. a, b
2. c
3. For the graph of $y = 4$, look for a horizontal line through $y = 4$; for the graph of $x + 2$, the line must include points (2, 0) and (0, 2). The solution is (-2, 4).
4. d
5. b
6. the coefficient of x is 2; the coefficient of y is 1
7. For the graph of $y = x + 4$, the line must include these points: (0, 4) and (-2, 2). For the graph of $y = -x + 10$, the line must include these points: (0, 10) and (10, 0). The solution is: $x = 3$ and $y = 7$

page 56
1. $x = 4$; $y = -1$
2. $x = \frac{4}{3}$; $y = -3$
3. $x = 14$; $y = -2$
4. $x = \frac{1}{4}$; $y = \frac{1}{3}$
5. $x = 7$; $y = 14$
6. $x = -\frac{1}{2}$; $y = 6$

7. $x = \frac{1}{2}$; $y = \frac{1}{3}$
8. $x = 5$; $y = 2$
9. $x = -3$; $y = \frac{1}{5}$
10. $x = -2$; $y = 3$

page 57
1. 4 and 12
2. Maxie is 8; Julia is 10
3. Maxwell is 40; son Maxwell Jr is 10
4. Alison is 36; Nelson is 14
5. May is 12; April is 18
6. Larry is 15; Moe is 5
7. instructor is 27; youngest student is 7

page 58
1. high school students = 8; other customers = 10
2. electrician: $50/hr; assistant: $25/hr
3. d
4. $x = \frac{1}{2}$; $y = -1$
5. $x = 8$; $y = 31$

Functions (pages 60-74)

pages 60-61
1. yes (because there is one specific output for each input)
2. yes
3. no
4. yes
5. no
6. a. yes; b. $y = 2$
7. no
8. yes
9. no
10. a. no; b. $x = 2$
11. no (because there is more than one output for a given input)
12. yes
13. no
14. yes
15. yes
16. yes

pages 62-63
1. Answers will vary. Make sure the points satisfy the equation.
2. Graphs should show parabola opening up at top, going through points on table
3. $f(0) = 2$; $f(-1) = 0$; $f(x + 1) = 2(x + 2) + 2 = 2x + 4$

4. Parabola opens downward with high point at (0, -2)

5. The graph (A) of the function should include points (0, -1); (1, 1); (4, 3); and (9, 5).

6. The graph (B) of the function should include points (-2, 6); (-1, 0); (0, -4); (1, -6); and (2, -6) (3, -4); (4, 0).

7. The graph (C) of the function should include points (-1, $\frac{1}{3}$); (0, 1); (1, 3); and (2, 9).

page 64

1. yes
2. yes (because there is one specific output for each input)
3. yes
4. yes
5. no
6. yes
7. yes
8. no
9. yes
10. no

pages 65-66-67

1. 150 m/hr and 250 m/hr
2. c
3. f
4. $14\frac{2}{3}$ hours—$6\frac{1}{3}$ by plane and $8\frac{1}{3}$ by train
5. a
6. a
7. c, d
8. a, c

page 68

1. yes; y = 3x – 9
2. no
3. no; the graph of the relationship is not a straight line
4. no; the graph of a linear function is a straight line
5. yes; y = 2x + 4
6. yes; the graph of the relationship is a straight line
7. no

page 69

1. b
2. $\frac{2}{3}$
3. a

page 70

1. b
2. b
3. x = 3
4. b
5. 2
6. The line must include points (0, -2) and (1, 0).

page 71

1. The line must start at (0, 40) and pass through (10, 90).
2. The line must include points (0, 6) and (4, 1).
3. y = -3x – 5

page 72

1. 7 hours
2. They will meet in 4 hours. They will meet when B has gone 24 k and A has gone 20 k.
3. y = -2x + 1
4. y = -$\frac{1}{2}$x + 7
5. The line must include points (-2, 0) and (-1, -3).
6. -3

page 73

1. b and d
2. The line must include points (0, 3) and (2, 0). The slope is -$\frac{3}{2}$.
3. y = mx – (m + 16)
4. slope = $\frac{5}{2}$; x-intercept = 0; y-intercept = 0

page 74

1. a
2. b
3. c
4. a
5. $\frac{3}{2}$
6. -$\frac{3}{4}$

Geometry (pages 76-110)

pages 76-77

1. yes
2. the same as
3. similar
4. none of these
5. stays the same
6. (-4, 8)
7. II
8. 15°
9. none of these
10. 104°, 20°, and 56°

11. (4, 4)
12. two parallel lines

pages 78-79

1. New line must include these points: (-4, 2) and (-2, 5).
2. a
3. A reflection of a line results in a line.
4. New line must include these points: (-2, 4) and -4, -1).
5. a
6. A reflection of a line results in a line.
7. Look for line rotated clockwise that includes points a_1 and b_1 as shown below.
8. a_1: (4, 4)
9. b_1: (-4, -1)
10. Look for a line translated to the right 2 units and down 3 units, parallel to the original line, that includes points c_1 and d_1 as shown below.
11. c_1: (-1, -3)
12. d_1: (2, -2)

page 80

1. no
2. p is a line and q is a line segment. Rotation of a figure does not change the figure.
3. Look for a line translated to the left 3 units and up 7 units, that includes points (-4, 3) and (1, 4).
4. a_1: (-4, 3)
5. b_1: (1, 4)
6. Look for a reflected line segment with endpoints (-2, -1) and (5, 1).
7. b
8. c

page 81

1. F; they will be (2, -5) and (9, -3)
2. F; it will stay at (-4, 5)
3. F; figures do not change to other figures during transformations
4. T
5. F; the distance

between parallel lines does not change during any transformation
6. F; endpoints will be in quadrant II, which has a -x value
7. F; point S will be located at (-6, 0)
8. T
9. T
10. F; during transformations, line segments remain the same length
11. F; parallel lines will never intersect
12. F; we cannot be sure of this because we are not told anything about the angle measurement or about the lengths or locations of the angle's sides

pages 82-83

1. Show a congruent angle with vertex at (-5, -3).
2. a
3. no
4. d
5. The vertex will stay at (-1, -2); the angle rotates counterclockwise until what was the top line points down parallel to the y-axis.
6. With vertex at (-2, -1), one ray passes through point (-1, 3) and the other ray passing through (-5, 1).
7. (-2, -1)
8. The vertex will be at (0, -5).
9. The vertex will be at (2, 4) and top ray will point left.
10. (2, 4)
11. c

pages 84-85

1. Points will be at a_1 = (2, 0) ; b_1 = (0, -4); c_1 = (2, 2) ; and d_1 = (0, -2).
2. c
3. two parallel lines
4. Line a_1 must include points (-5, -5) and

(2, -1). Line b_1 must include points (-5, -4) and (2, 0).
5. b
6. a
7. Line a_1 must include points (0, -1) and (5, 1); line b_1 must include (0, -4) and (5, -2).
8. (5, 1)
9. (0, -4)
10. Line c_1 must include points (-2, 3) and (3, 0). Line d_1 must include points (-2, 4) and (3, 1).
11. c
12. (3, 1)

pages 86-87
1. G, H, L, I
2. L
3. J
4. C, D, F

Answers for 5-9 will vary. Look for general, accurate descriptions of transformations.
5. To obtain second figure, figure has been reflected across a vertical line, rotated about -90° and translated.
6. To obtain the second figure, the figure has been translated to the right.
7. To obtain the second figure, the figure has been reflected across a vertical line and rotated about -90°.
8. To obtain the second figure, the figure has been reflected across a vertical line, and translated.
9. To obtain the second figure, the figure has been reflected across a horizontal line and translated.

pages 88-89
1. Figure A_1 coordinates will be (2, 4); (2, 1); (-3, 1); (-3, 2); (1, 2); (1, 4).
2. Figure A_2 coordinates will be (4, -2); (4, -5); (-1, -5); (-1, -4); (3, -4); (3, -2).

3. (1, -5)
4. yes
5. Figure B_1 coordinates will be (4, 5); (4, 1); (0, 2); (0, 3).
6. Figure B_2 coordinates will be (-4, 5); (-4, 1); (0, 2); (0, 3).
7. (-4, 1)
8. yes
9. no; after rotation and translation, the longest legs differ in length
10. no; after rotation and translation, the longest bases differ in length
11. yes
12. yes
13. no; after reflection and translation, figure F proves to be longer than figure K

pages 90-91
1. Show new figure at A_1 (1, -4); B_1 (3, -4); C_1 (2, 1); D_1 (-1, -1)
2. (2, 1)
3. Show original figure at P (5, 3); Q (5, -2); R (2, -3); S (2, 2) and new figure at P_1: (-3, 3); Q_1 (-3, -2); R_1 (0, -3); S_1 (0, 2).
4. It is the same.
5. Placement of figures may vary. One possibility is F_1 (-4, 0); G_1 (0, 4); H_1 (4, 0)
6. I and II
7. Check for the figure at the given coordinates.
8. translation: +2 in relation to the x-axis and -3 in relation to the y-axis

pages 92-93
Explanations for 1-7 will vary.
1. yes; a circle (or sphere) will stay proportional when the radius changes
2. yes; all corresponding angles are equal and all side measurements for D are $\frac{1}{2}$ of the corresponding side measurements for C
3. no; the changes in

measurements are not proportional from one figure to the other
4. no; the changes in measurements are not proportional from one figure to the other
5. yes; all measurements in I are 80% of the measurements in J
6. yes; with 90° rotation around point (-4, -2) and translation +9 in relation to the x-axis and -2 in relation to the y-axis, figure C looks similar to figure D. In addition, the two congruent angles in the two figures and the proportional sizes of the legs confirm its similarity.
7. no; Figure F looks like figure E reflected and translated, but they are not similar. The lengths of their sides are not proportional.

pages 94-95
Answers will vary, depending on how the animals follow the paths. Here are some possible answers:
1. 420°
2. 328°
3. 360°
4. 480°
5. HL
6. NC
7. SAS
8. AAS

pages 96-97
1. a
2. a
3. b
4. b
5. b
6. c
7. b
8. a
9. b
10. a

page 98
1. The angles marked congruent in the diagram add to 90°.

Therefore, the angles in the square are 180° – 90°, which equals 90°.
2. by SSS rule (side-side-side)
3. The area of the triangle is $\frac{1}{2}$ base times height or, for the four triangles, $4(\frac{1}{2}ab)$.
4. Expanding (FOIL) and simplifying

page 99
1. by Pythagorean Theorem in triangle XYZ
2. given
3. substitution
4. taking positive square roots of both sides
5. by SSS rule (side-side-side)
6. corresponding parts of congruent figures are congruent
7. definition of a right triangle

page 100
A. 15 m	F. 17 m
B. 9 m	G. 13 m
C. $\sqrt{11}$ m	H. $20\sqrt{10}$ m
D. 4 m	I. 6 m
E. 10 m	

page 101
1. Sue
2. $\sqrt{11}$ ft (or 3.3 ft)
3. 3 ft

pages 102-103
1. 260 m
2. 200 m

pages 104-105
1. $\sqrt{313}$
2. $\sqrt{241}$
3. 13
4. 51 m; slide length = $\sqrt{545}$
5. 10
6. yes (150 ft); slide length = 170 ft
7. 17
8. $6\sqrt{5}$

pages 106-107
1. V = 5,274 cm^3
2. h = 1.5 in
3. h = 15 cm
4. V = 434.7 in^3
5. V = 4,710 cm^3
6. V (cone) = 113 cm^3;

V (ice cream) = 134 cm³; total V = approx. 247 cm³

7. V = 317.9 cm³
8. V = 453.4 cm³
9. V = 3,633.3 in³
10. r = 20 cm
11. V = 28.26 cm³
12. h = 20 in
13. r = 1.5 cm

pages 108-109

A. 7.15π in³
B. 5,827.63π cm³
C. 52.41π cm³
D. 1,333.33π cm³
E. 10,666.67π mm³
F. 121.5π in³
G. 3.9π in³
H. 7,776π mm³
I. 2,246.88π cm³
J. 67.54π cm³
K. 9.15π in³
L. 12,884.8π mm³
M. 1.9π in³

Order of size: H. foosball, E. ping pong ball, L. golf ball, M. billiard ball, C. tennis ball, G. T-ball, J. baseball, A. softball, K. whiffle ball, D. volleyball, F. soccer ball, I. basketball, B. water polo ball

page 110

1. 61.25 π in³
2. The volumes are the same: 320π cm³
3. 21.195 in³
4. the spherical container
5. Hudson's; 167
6. yes
7. 11,725π cm³

Statistics and Probability (pages 112-126)

page 112

1. d   4. b
2. c   5. d
3. a   6. d

page 113

1. Look for graph labeled with

distances along vertical axis and years along horizontal axis. Look for dots placed to match data.
2. Look for a straight line sloping up from left to right through a cloud of points.
3. true
4. true

pages 114-115

1. Look for dots placed to match data.
2. Placement of lines may vary. Look for a straight line slanting up from left to right, with a generally equivalent portion of data above and below the line.
3. b
4. Look for dots placed to match data.
5. Placement of lines may vary. Look for a straight line slanting down from left to right, with a generally equivalent portion of data above and below the line.
6. c

pages 116-117

1. number of injuries with no previous competition this year
2. b
3. c
4. zero
5. true
6. true
7. quadratic (or parabola)

page 118

1. Look for dots placed to match data.
2. Look for a line that heads upward from left to right but begins to level off.
3. Answers will vary. One explanation

may be that a fish will probably grow faster when it's younger, but that the growth would level off with time.
4. 2

page 119

1. There had been 2 firings before any additional gunpowder was brought in.
2. $\frac{3}{2}$ or 1.5
3. y = $\frac{3}{2}$ x + 2 (or y = $\frac{1}{5}$x + 2)
4. no
5. quadratic (or parabola)

page 120

1. Look for dots placed to match data.
2. Look for a straight line starting at the origin and sloping up from left to right.
3. time per lap
4. at the origin: no laps, no time elapsed
5. yes

page 121

1. 7$\frac{1}{2}$
2. 10; the y-intercept is 10, which means that a student could expect to get a grade of 10% with zero hours of study and homework
3. y = 10x + 10
4. the rate of change is the slope, 10; this means that for every additional hour of homework and study, the test score rises by 10%

page 122

1. Look for graph to be correctly labeled with times along y-axis, with numbers 0 to 12, and with average heights along the x-axis,

numbered from 66 to 74 or greater. Look for dots placed to match data.
2. Look for a straight line sloping up from left to right.
3. shoe size per inch of height
4. No, negative shoe size or small heights are not realistic for this real-life situation.

page 123

1. c (Students may draw different conclusions from these data and could also argue for b.)
2. Completed table: % sick: weekend days 17%; weekdays 19%; % energetic: weekend days 83%; weekdays 81%
3. c

page 124

1. 0.02
2. 0
3. 0.03
4. 0.04
5. 0.17
6. 0.35
7. 0.25
8. 0.15
9. no
10. yes
11. True
12. Jill

page 125

1. b
2. c
3. c
4. b

page 126

1. Completed table: students who said yes: 43%; students who said no: 57%; teachers who said yes: 52%; teachers who said no: 48%
2. b
3. c